# Missions
## *Reaching the Unreached & Planting Churches*

Dr. Alvin A. Low

Missions (Reaching the Unreached & Planting Churches)
Copyright © 2009 by Dr. Alvin A. Low.
(E-mail: AlvinLow98@yahoo.com) All rights reserved.

Published by
ACTS International
2715 Clapton Drive
Colorado Springs, Colorado 80920
United States of America
www.actsinternational.net

Printed in U.S.A., 2009.



Scripture quotations, unless otherwise marked, are taken from the "NIV" -- the *Holy Bible, New International Version* ®, Copyright © 1973, 1978, 1984 by International Bible Society. Used by permission of Zondervan Publishing House. All rights reserved.

Scripture quotations marked "NASB" are taken from the *New American Standard Bible* ®, Copyright © 1960, 1962, 1963, 1968, 1971, 1972, 1973, 1975, 1977, 1995 by The Lockman Foundation. Used by permission. All rights reserved.

# Table of Contents

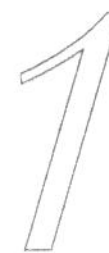

# What is Missions?

**Introduction**

There has been a lot of confusion on "what is missions?" What activities constitute missionary activities? If we do not define what missions is, then we are shooting in the dark. Ask the average church goers, and they will give various answers, such as:

- sharing the Gospel
- discipleship
- the Great Commission
- going overseas to share the Gospel
- changing lives at all levels of society
- compassion work
- short-term missions
- building houses for the homeless
- feeding hungry children
- planting churches.

The list can go on. If we do not understand what missions is, we will most probably miss the target.

Before we proceed, let us clarify the difference between "mission" and "missions" (mission with an "s").

George Peters gives an excellent distinction between the two terms.  According to him, mission "refers to the total biblical assignment of the church of Jesus Christ.  It is a comprehensive term including the upward, inward and outward ministries of the church." [1]  We will clarify the definition of "missions" in the subsequent paragraphs.

In order to define missions, let us return to the first missionary journey of Paul and see what he did.  This is a safe (and right) place to start.

## Paul's Missions

The Book of Acts records the advancement of the gospel into other lands, and it offers insight into apostolic missions.  Even though the *description* of what took place cannot become a *prescription* for modern day missions, it is nevertheless helpful to gain an understanding of what the apostles did in their missionary journeys.

What did Paul do that would constitute "missions"?

Paul Beals has written accurately about Paul's missions model in his book, *A People for His Name*.[2]  He summarizes Paul's missions as follows:

---

[1] George W. Peters, *A Biblical Theology of Missions* (Chicago, IL: Moody Press, 1972), 11.
[2] Paul A Beals, *A People for His Name* (Pasadena, CA: William Carey Library, 1995), 15-24.

| Evangelizing the Unreached | Equipping the Disciples | Establishing Local Churches |
|---|---|---|
| Acts 14:21 | Acts 14:22 | Acts 14:23 |
| Preaching the gospel Making disciples | Strengthening Encouraging | Appointing Committing |
| Proclaiming | Perfecting | Planting |

## Evangelizing the Unreached

Paul and Barnabas set forth for their first missionary journey (Acts 13:1-14:28), from Antioch to Salamis and Paphos (in Cyprus), and then to Perga, Antioch, Iconium, Lystra, and coming to Derbe,[3] we are told that they *"preached the good news in that city and won a large number of disciples."* (Acts 14:21)

The word for "preach" in Acts 14:21 is *euangelizo* meaning "to proclaim good tidings. *Euangelizo* is used fifty-four times in the New Testament. The related word *euangelion*, "good news" or "gospel," is used seventy-six times in the New Testament. There are other words used for the communication of the gospel in the New Testament:

- *kerusso* – proclaim (Acts 8:5)
- *martureo* – testify, witness (Acts 26:22-23)

David Hesselgrave lists thirteen additional terms: *syngcheo* (confound, Acts 9:22); *symbibazo* (prove, Acts 9:22); *dialegeomai* (declare, Acts 9:27); *syzeteo* (dispute, Acts 9:29); *laleo* (speak, Acts 9:29); *dialegomai* (reason with, Acts 18:4); *peitho* (persuade, Acts 18:4); *noutheteo* (admonish, warn, Acts 20:31); *katecho* (inform, instruct, Acts 21:21-24); *deomai* (beg, beseech, 2 Cor. 5:20); *elengcho*

---

[3] Gaius became a disciple of Christ in Derbe, most probably during this time (Acts 20:4).

(reprove, 2 Tim. 4:2); *epitimao* (rebuke, 2 Tim. 4:2); *parakaleo* (exhort, urge, 1 Peter 2:11).[4]

*Paul's First Missionary Journey*

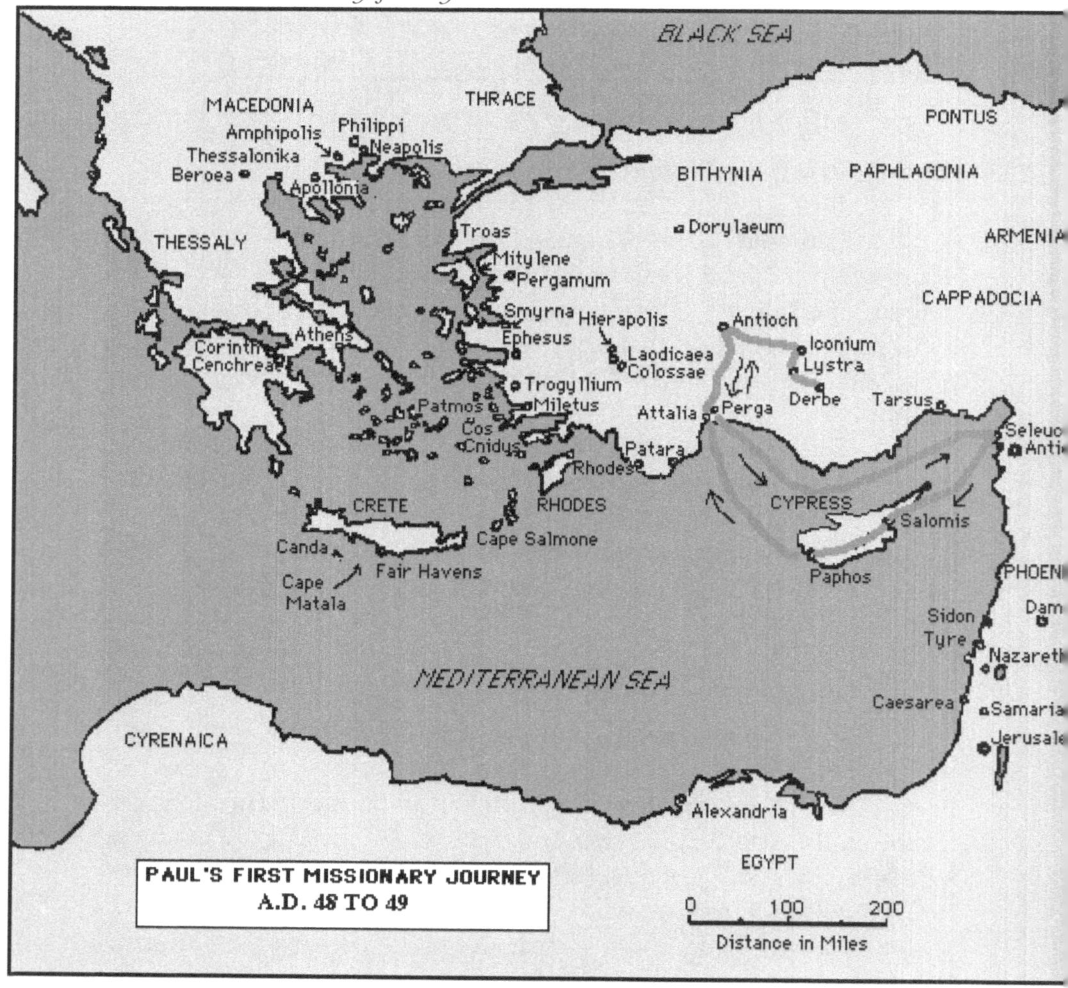


---

[4] David J. Hesselgrave, *Communicating Christ Cross-Culturally* (Grand Raid, MI: Zondervan Publishing House, 1978), 2-21. Also quoted in Paul Beals', 17

The content of the "good news" they preached is defined in 1 Corinthians 15:1-7:

*Now, brothers, I want to remind you of the gospel I preached to you, which you received and on which you have taken your stand. By this gospel you are saved, if you hold firmly to the word I preached to you. Otherwise, you have believed in vain. For what I received I passed on to you as of first importance: {3 Or you at the first} that Christ died for our sins according to the Scriptures, that he was buried, that he was raised on the third day according to the Scriptures, and that he appeared to Peter, {5 Greek Cephas} and then to the Twelve. After that, he appeared to more than five hundred of the brothers at the same time, most of whom are still living, though some have fallen asleep. Then he appeared to James, then to all the apostles.*

The "gospel" they preached concerns:

- Christ's death for our sins according to the Scriptures. (His burial authenticates his death.)
- Christ's resurrection on the third day according to the Scriptures. (His appearances authenticate His resurrection.)

In preaching this gospel of Jesus Christ, Paul summoned the listeners to respond to this good news. He called them …

- *to turn from these worthless things to the living God* (Acts 14:15)
- *to repent* (Acts 17:30)
- *to repent and turn to God and prove their repentance by their deeds* (Acts 26:20)

In Derbe, Paul and Barnabas *"preached the good news in that city and won a large number of disciples."* (Acts 14:21)  Paul Beals says,

The expression, "and won… disciples" (*matheteusantes*), is the same word used in Matthew 28:19 "and *make disciples* of all nations" (*matheteusante0*). Both passages distinctly teach that when a person hears the gospel and believes it, he becomes a disciple. Becoming a disciple of Christ is not dependent on "discipling" subsequent to placing one's faith in Christ. The kingdom is not made up of two kinds of believers – some who are disciples and some who are not.[5]

The first component of "missions" is the preaching of the gospel to win disciples for Christ.

## Equipping the Disciples

The second component of missions is the equipping or the strengthening of the disciples. Paul and Barnabas retraced their journey when they *returned to Lystra, Iconium and Antioch, strengthening the disciples and encouraging them to remain true to the faith. "We must go through many hardships to enter the kingdom of God," they said.* (Acts 14:21b-22)

> The word translated "strengthening" (*episterizontes*) means "to build up with additional (*epi*) strength." The term is found in the New Testament only in Acts 14:22; 15:32, 41; and 18:23. In each instance it refers to building up believers in the faith. In fact, Paul's two subsequent journeys started with "strengthening" ministries among the churches. At the beginning of his second journey, Paul "went through Syria and Cilicia, *strengthening* the churches" (Acts 15:41). After furloughing in Antioch, he initiated his third journey "and traveled from place to place throughout the region of Galatia and Phrygia, *strengthening* all the disciples" (Acts 18:23).
> Second, the apostles went about "encouraging" the believers (*parakalountes*). This term conveys the thought of pleading, exhorting, or beseeching. A sense of urgency prevailed. Paul wrote to the Philippian church, "I *plead*

---

[5] Paul Beals, 18.

with Euodia and I *plead* with Syntyche to agree with each other in the Lord" (Phil. 4:2).  Again Paul reminds Timothy, "As I *urged* you when I went into Macedonia, stay there in Ephesus..." (1 Tim. 1:3).  The encouragement to remain true to the faith was doubly urgent because of the hardships that come in the Christian life.[6]

Paul encouraged the believers not only through his personal visits, but also through his letters.  After the first missionary journey, Paul wrote the Book of Galatians because the Judaizers discredited the apostleship of Paul and preached a substitute gospel. Paul wrote to defend his apostleship and his message of justification and sanctification by grace.  Paul wrote the letter to encourage the believers to stay true to the gospel of grace.

## Establishing Local Churches

The third component of "missions" is to establish local churches.

*Paul and Barnabas appointed elders for them in each church and, with prayer and fasting, committed them to the Lord, in whom they had put their trust.* (Acts 14:23)  Paul and Barnabas have preached the gospel, and won the disciples, strengthen the disciples, and then they formed the disciples into local churches with appointed elders.

First, the apostles *appointed (cheirotonesantes) elders* in each church.  This is an intriguing compound word "that originally meant to vote by show of hands."  This term does not mean "ordain" in the sense in which it is understood today.  Paul used this word later when he said of Titus, "What is more, he *was chosen* by the church to accompany us as we carry the offering..." (2 Cor. 8:19).  No explicit evidence appears in the text, but circumstances

---

[6] Paul Beals, 19.

indicate that these men were chosen as elders by the believers. Then they were set apart by the apostles for their duties.[7]

The second action the apostles took was to *commit these churches and their leaders* to the Lord in whom they had trusted. The term "committed" (*parethento*) is the verb *paratithemi* (v. 23). The form in which it occurs (middle voice) means "to commit someone or something to another for protection or keeping." For example, the Lord Jesus said, "Father, into your hands I *commit* my spirit" (Luke 23:46). On a later occasion in Paul's ministry, the apostle said to the Ephesian elders, "Now I *commit* you yo God and to the word of his grace…" (Acts 20:32). And what a solemn event it was. This commitment of the churches was "with prayer and fasting." Paul cast them entirely on God for their personal and corporate life. He would not have them tied to his apron strings. He visited them, wrote to them, and sent some of the missionary team to encourage them, but Paul never made the churches dependent on him.[8]

## Conclusion

The *sine qua non* of missions is therefore
- evangelizing the unreached,
- equipping the disciples, and
- establishing local churches (Acts 14:21-23).

If these components are not present in our missionizing, we are not involved in biblical missions in the truest sense.[9]

---

[7] Paul Beals, 21-22.
[8] Paul Beals, 22.
[9] Paul Beals, 23.

Missions: where the three
components intersect.

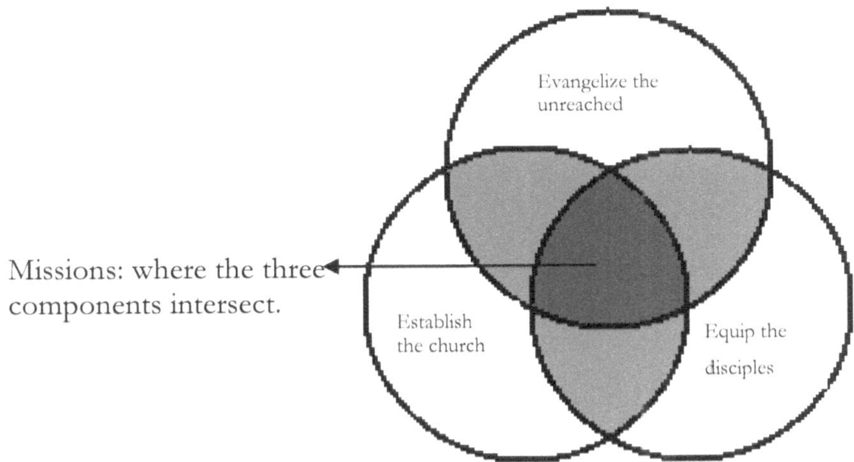



George Peters defines missions (mission with an "s") as "the sending forth of authorized persons beyond the borders of the New Testament church and her immediate gospel influence to proclaim the gospel of Jesus Christ in gospel-destitute areas, to win converts from other faiths or non-faiths to Jesus Christ, and to establish functioning, multiplying local congregations who will bear the fruit of Christianity in that community and to that country."[10] Missions therefore does not refer to the redemptive activities of the church within the societies *where the church is found*. Missions refers to the redemptive activity of the church within societies where the church is <u>not</u> found.[11]

## Assignment

Evaluate your church missions program.  Do the missions programs reflect the *sine qua non* of the church's mission?

---

[10] George W. Peters, *A Biblical Theology of Missions*, 11.
[11] Ralph Winter, "What is Mission" in *Mission Frontiers*, July 1987

*2*

# Who is a Missionary?

Equally confusing is the question, "Who is a missionary?" Ask any church goers, and they will respond with different answers, such as:

A missionary is someone who...

- shares the Gospel
- preaches the Good News
- goes overseas to share the Gospel
- builds houses for the poor
- feeds the hungry
- disciples new believers
- is suffering for Christ
- takes care of a missionary guest house

Again, the list can go on. It includes people who do a whole spectrum of activities. Who then exactly is a missionary?

Let me begin with an example. If I ask you, "who is a medical doctor?" You will possibly answer, "he/she is a person who has been trained in the medical field, and is having his/her medical practice normally in a hospital or a clinic." The answer comprises a few elements:

1. He/she has been trained in the area of his/her expertise.
2. He/she is practicing "medicine", that is the "nature" of his/her job – to "heal" the sick.
3. He/she is doing his/her work in a "place" – normally the hospital or a clinic. Of course, he/she can practice medicine in a place other than a hospital or clinic (such as a classroom), but the hospital or the clinic is the "normal" place of his/her work. His/her place is also where the "sick" are. Therefore, he/she has a target "people group" – the "sick."

In order to answer the question, "who is a missionary," it seems best to find out
1. if he/she has been called and trained to do the job (just as in the case of the medical doctor)
2. if he/she is doing the work of a missionary. In other words, we need to know the "nature" of his/her work.
3. if he/she is working in a "place" defined as the "mission field." The nature of his/her assignment and the place where he/she is stationed are inseparable. Both are needed to define who he/she is. Since the place is where the "people" live, is there a specific "people group"[12] he/she is trying to reach.

Over the years, there has been a dilution in the use of the words "missionary," "missions or missionary work" and "mission field." Very often, the word "missionary" has been used to refer to anyone who has joined a "mission" organization. It does not

---

[12] A "people group" is defined as "a significantly large sociological grouping of individuals who perceive themselves to have a common affinity for one another, because of their language, religion, ethnicity, residence, occupation, class or caste situation, etc, or a combination of these." (Edward R. Dayton, *That Everyone May Hear* [Manrovia: Mission Advanced Research and Communication Center, 1980] 25-26.)

matter whether he/she is a teacher or an accountant. As long as he/she is in a so-called "missions" organization, he/she is called a "missionary." Or some people go to the extreme of saying that every Christian is a missionary. But is it?

How about the "mission field"? Any place beyond a person's shore has been called a "mission field." He/she may be serving as an English teacher, or an administrator, or a plumber for a so-called "mission" organization, and so long as he/she is stationed overseas or beyond his/her own border, he/she is therefore "in" the mission field. But is it?

Let us go back to the basics.

## What is a mission field?

What is a mission field? Let us look at Paul. What constituted a mission field for Paul?

Paul considered a mission field as ...

- a place where Christ's name is not known. Paul wanted to *"preach the gospel where Christ was not known"* (Rom. 15:20). In the early church, people in most places had yet to know Jesus Christ.
- A people-group who has yet to know Christ. The "where" of Romans 15:20 is certainly a place with people living in it. Therefore Paul could also have been thinking of the people-group in a particular place who had yet to know Christ.

What is the difference between the Great Commission (Matt. 28:18-20) and the mission field we have just defined? The Great Commission is given to all believers. We are commanded to "make disciples" of all nations. The Great Commission emphasizes the command and the process of making disciples. The central command of the Great Commission is to "make disciples," and the process is to "go", "baptize", and "teach" the believers to observe all that Jesus commanded.  The people group is defined as all "nationalities" or all "ethnic" groups.

The mission field is defined in terms of a place or a people-group.  Within any nation, there is a people-group which has yet to come to know Christ.  While we are commanded to make disciples of all nations, we are technically not involved in missions when we are stationed in a place or among a people-group who have already heard the Gospel or who have access to the Gospel message.  "Making disciples" is not missionary work.  It is "disciple-making" work.  Missionary work involves the making of disciples, but the reverse may not be necessary true.  I am not saying that "disciple-making" is not important.  It is important.  Christ commanded it.  But "disciple-making" does not constitute missionary work.  Otherwise, all of us would have to be called "missionaries" as long as we obey the Great Commission.  Specifically, the mission field refers to a place or a people-group who has never heard of the Gospel.

Missionary work focuses on the places and people-groups where Christ has yet to be known.  It has therefore a narrow focus.

Unfortunately, we have defined missions in very general terms to include everyone who is doing evangelism in his own backyard, or among his own colleagues, or among a people who already has access to the Gospel. Evangelism is sharing the good news of Jesus Christ, but doing evangelism among a people-group or in a place where the Gospel message is readily available is technically not "missions." The dilution of the "focus" of missions does great harms to the church and the missionary enterprise. Once the focus is diluted, there is always a tendency to concentrate on the peripheral to the peril of millions of souls yet to know the Name of Jesus.

**What is the nature of the missionary work?**

The nature of medical work is to "heal" the sick through prognosis and dispensing the appropriate medicine. The nature of his work is inseparable from his/her profession.

The same applies to a "missionary." What is the nature of his/her work that defines him/her as a "missionary" distinct from other callings? From chapter one, we define the *sine qua non* of missions as

- evangelizing the unreached,
- equipping the disciples, and
- establishing local churches (Acts 14:21-23).

The missionary task involves…

1. Going to the unreached peoples and areas of the world where Christ has not been named, or as George Peters defines it, "gospel-destitute areas." I prefer to call it "unreached" peoples and places where they have not heard of the Name of Jesus, neither do they have churches and Christians within their vicinity where the Gospel is accessible to them. In order to reach the unreached, sometimes, it is necessary to cross

geographical borders and/or cultural and religious lines. But it may not be the case. For example, our church planters in Nepal know the language/s of the unreached peoples in the various mountains and valleys, and they venture into these mountains and valleys to preach the Good News. There are no linguistic barriers even though there are geographical challenges. Similarly, Paul and Barnabas (and the early disciples) spoke Aramaic, and when they went on their first missionary journey, they spoke Aramaic, not another foreign language. In fact, there are no New Testament records of any of the apostles ever using another language to reach the unreached except the Apostle Thomas who went to India according to early church history.[13] They are nevertheless "missionaries" because they went to the "unreached" and preached the Good News.

2. The second component of the missionary task is to strengthen, encourage, or equip the disciples.

3. The third component of the missionary task is to gather the disciples to form new churches. The consequence of disciples-making is always the planting of new churches because disciples do not grow alone. Paul planted new churches in places he evangelized. The churches are continually built up so that they become reproducing churches.

## Who is a missionary?

Now we are ready to define a missionary. The words "mission" and "missionary" come from the Latin word *mitto* (I send). Since the Bible was not written in Latin, but in Greek and Hebrew, the equivalent word would be "apostle" (*apostolos* in

---

[13] Bob Finley, *Reformation in Foreign Missions* (Xulon Press, 2005), 15-21.

Greek) which means "sent one." The verb *apostello* has the idea of being sent.[14]

A missionary is someone who

1. has been called and trained in missionary work. The apostles were called by Jesus Christ; they were trained by Jesus for three years before being sent.
2. is laboring among a people-group or in a place where Christ has not yet been known by
   - proclaiming the Gospel of Jesus Christ, <u>and</u>
   - equipping the disciples, <u>and</u>
   - establishing new churches.

George Peters defines a missionary as "a Christian messenger of the gospel of Jesus Christ, sent forth by the authority of the Lord and the church to cross national borders and/or cultural and religious lines in order to occupy new frontiers for Christ, to preach the gospel of redemption in Christ Jesus unto the salvation of people, to make disciples and to establish functioning and evangelizing Christian churches according to the command of Christ and the example of the apostles."[15]

Not every Christian is a missionary in the strict sense of the word. Neither is a person who joins a so-called "missions organization" to be called a missionary if he/she does not satisfy the requirements above. Usually he/she is involved in some other activities which can be classified as follows:

1. Missions support: Missions support that directly contribute toward the missionary task such as training national church planters and pastoral leaders for discipleship and church planting.

---

14 C. Gordon Olson, *What in the World is God doing?* (Cedar Knolls, NJ: Global Gospel Publishers, 1993), 10.
15 George W. Peters, *A Biblical Theology of Missions*, 248-49.

2.  Ministries:  I would classify all other "activities" which do not directly or indirectly contribute toward the making of disciples AND the planting of churches among an unreached people group as "ministries" not "missions."  They are good "ministries" (such as educational services -- teaching English in the university, or teaching children, or building schools, or social services such as feeding the hungry, clothing the naked, ministering to the physical needs of the refugees, or transformative services which seeks to transform the society through law and order, and the pursuit of justice.)  Those are worthy causes, but they are not "missionary work" in its strictest definition. The purpose of the narrow definition is to stay biblical and to drive the church back to its core, to focus on what is needed to be done.

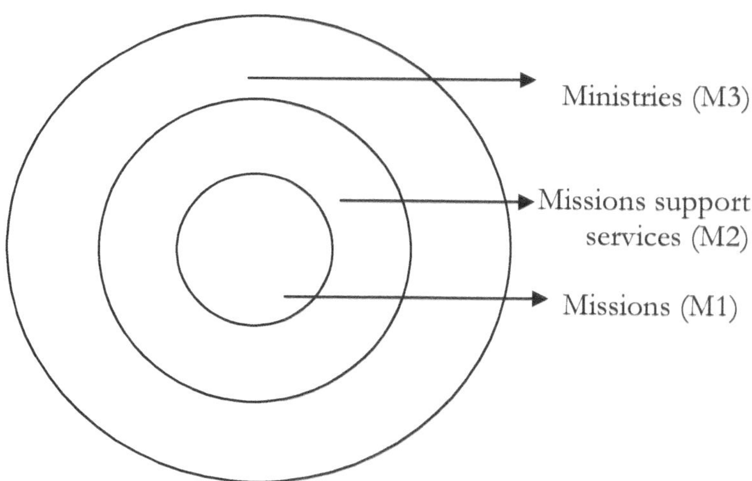

**Assignment:**

How many of your missionaries are involved in the *sine qua non* of missions:

- evangelizing the unreached,
- equipping the disciples, and
- establishing new churches?

# What are the Implications?

## Introduction

What are the implications of the definitions of "missions" and "missionaries" of the first two chapters? The implications are far reaching. For too long, churches, ministries, and donors do not focus on the core of missions, partly because they simply don't know what missions is all about, and the seminaries are not teaching it, and the churches are not calling us back to the core business of missions.

## Manpower allocation

The confusion on what missions is all about has resulted in personnel dislocation. If our focus is diluted, or if we are convinced that every Christian is a missionary, then there is no need to focus on the unreached peoples or places of the world. The result of the dilution of focus has done great harm to the cause of missions. Many who consider themselves as missionaries are laboring among those peoples who are already evangelized, or who have access-to the gospel or to a church. I am not minimizing their work. They are doing good work. Unfortunately, the large pockets of people yet to be reached remain untouched.

Patrick Cate mentions "that about 80% of Christian workers minister to the 7.6% of the world population who speak English. Yet many people-groups and areas have no workers. About three billion out of six billion people on earth do not live where they can attend a church to hear the gospel in their language and culture. Ninety-seven percent of the least-reached peoples are in, or come from, the 10/40 Window – from 10° to 40° latitude

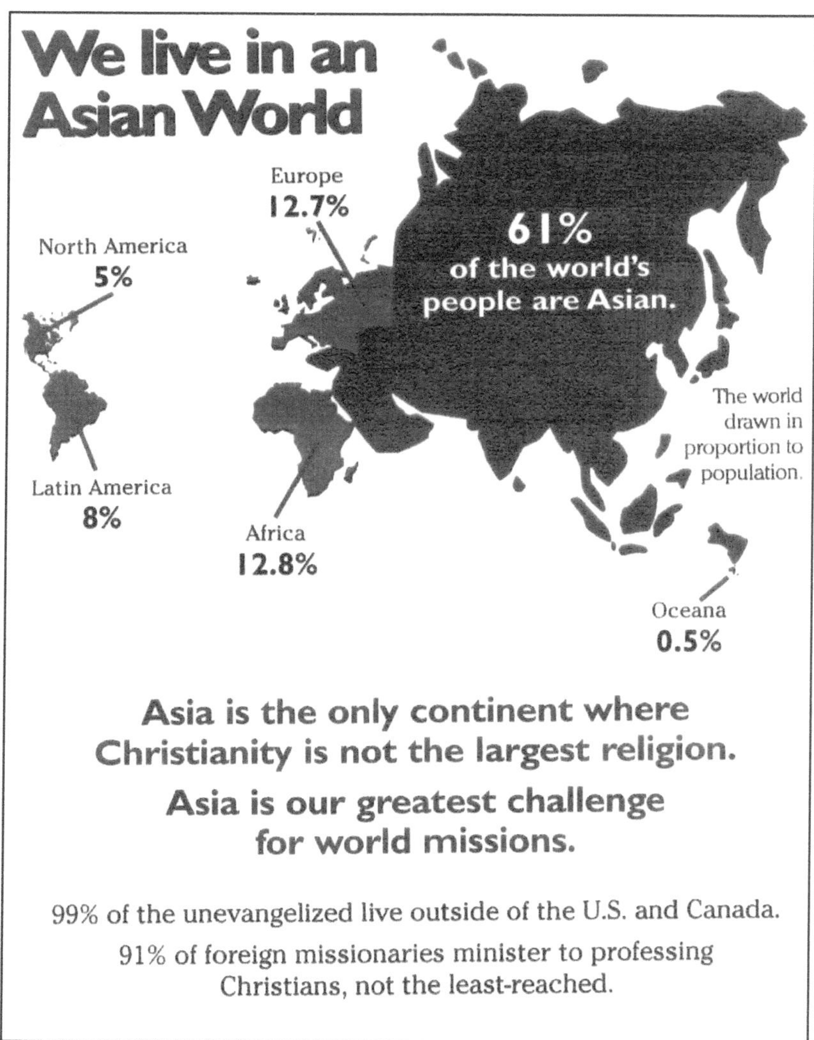

above the equator, across Africa and Asia. Most of those who live in, or come from, the Window do not have a reasonable chance of hearing the gospel in their lifetime. Most who live outside of the Window do."[16]

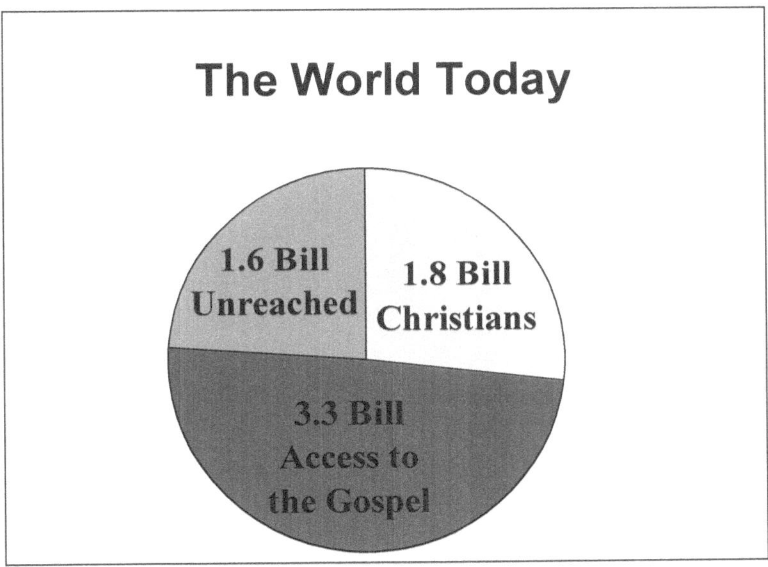



---

[16] Patrick O. Cate, *Through God's Eyes* (Pasadena, CA: William Carey Library, 2004), 60.

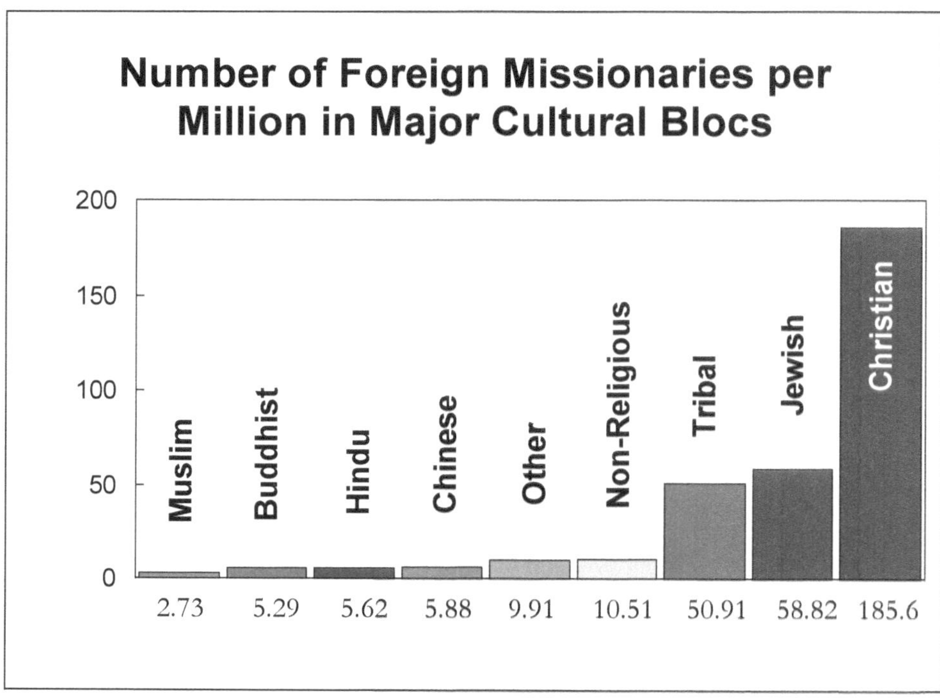


## Missionomics

The second area that is severely affected by the confusion over what missions is is that of missions-finances, or missionomics. This is a new term specifically coined to refer to the study of financial investments by churches, organizations and foundations in missions.

How much of the church's support goes to missions (M1) which support a person who is "called, equipped, and sent forth by the authority of the Lord and the church to cross national, and/or cultural and religious barriers in order to occupy new frontiers for Christ, to preach the gospel of redemption in Christ Jesus unto the salvation of people, to make disciples and to establish functioning and evangelizing Christian churches according to the command of Christ and the examples of the apostles"?[17]

How much of our support goes toward missions support services (M2) which support the frontline soldiers? Or is a majority of our funding going toward ministries unrelated to the core?

Let us look at the budget of one local church (First Baptist Church of Marshville)[18]. The church has the following "missions budget":

**FIRST BAPTIST CHURCH OF MARSHVILLE**
**2008 MISSION ENDOWMENT BUDGET**
**AVAILABLE FUNDS**
Disbursement from Stegall Endowment State Missions Fund $15,000
Disbursement from Stegall Endowment Home Missions Fund $15,000
Disbursement from Stegall Endowment Foreign Missions Fund $15,000
Carried Forward from 2007 $800
**TOTAL MISSIONS FUNDING AVAILABLE $45,800**

**PROPOSED ALLOCATIONS**
Missions through Congregational Ministry $5,200
Missions through Local Partnerships $20,600
Missions through Global Partnerships $20,000
**TOTAL PROPOSED MISSIONS BUDGET $45,800**

**MISSIONS THROUGH CONGREGATIONAL MINISTRY**
**Benevolence Fund**
Allows our church to provide direct assistance for individuals with short-term, immediate needs $1000

---

[17] George W. Peters, *A Biblical Theology of Missions*, 248-49.
[18] The figures are exact as given on their web site www.fbcmarshville.org

**Camp Grants**
Helps persons affiliated with First Baptist Church attend church-sponsored camps and retreats $1200
**Communication Outreach**
Provides resources that allow our congregation to reach out to the community through ads, signs, banners and mailings $500
**Leadership Training**
Makes it possible to send members of our congregation to training events that equip them for more effective ministry in the church and community $500
**Mission Trip**
Provides funds for adults and/or youth affiliated with First Baptist to participate in a short-term missions trip $1000
**Vacation Bible School**
Helps our church make a more significant impact in the community through our annual VBS by providing additional resources for supplies and promotion $1,000
**TOTAL MISSIONS THROUGH CONGREGATIONAL MINISTRY $5,200**


**MISSIONS THROUGH LOCAL PARTNERSHIPS**
**Community Health Services** $500
**Health Quest of Union County**
A program sponsored by Union Regional Medical Center that provides
prescription drugs to those who otherwise could not afford them $1200
**H.E.L.P. Crisis Pregnancy Center**
Provides support and encouragement to single pregnant women $1700
**Hospice of Union County**
Provides support and assistance for persons and their families who are facing a terminal illness $3500
**New Life 91.9 (WRCM)**
Offers radio listeners in the Charlotte area a "family friendly" Christian station. A ministry of Columbia

International University, New Life 91.9 is listener supported. $500

**Operation Reach Out**

Volunteer program in Union County to provide for individuals in times of crisis $1500

**Regional AIDS Interfaith Network**

Provides care teams that minister to those with AIDS $500

**Union County Christmas Bureau**

Helps needy families provide their children with Christmas gifts $1200

**Union County Crisis Assistance Ministry**

Provides assistance to individuals in times of crisis $4000

**Union County Habitat for Humanity**

Provides adequate housing for those in need. Our contribution will be

earmarked to cover our church's participation in a Habitat building project. $2000

**Union County Homeless Shelter**

Provides year round shelter to homeless persons in Union County $2000

**Union County Turning Point**

Provides year round shelter to homeless persons in Union County $2000

**TOTAL MISSIONS THROUGH LOCAL PARTNERSHIPS $20,600**


**MISSIONS THROUGH GLOBAL PARTNERSHIPS**

**Baptist World Alliance**

Network of Baptist bodies around the world that coordinates evangelism,

training and response to human need $1,000

**Presson, Brian – Ministry Support**

Brian Presson and his family have served as missionaries in Thailand for a

number of years. Our funds are used to fund their work, to support Thai

evangelists, and to provide vital ministry supplies. $6000

**Presson, Brian – Family Support**
Brian's children attend an accredited, English-speaking school organized by a cooperating group of mission agencies. Our funds help defray tuition costs. $4000

**Threatt, Myles and Kristi**
Myles and Kristi Threatt are missionaries from the Marshville area who are serving in Thailand through the Pioneers mission agency. $6000

**Village of Hope**
*Village of Hope* is a project of CBF that provides housing, food and education for street children in Kiev, a city in the former Soviet Union $1500

**Wycliffe Bible Translators (JARRS)**
Translates and distributes scriptures throughout the world $1500

**TOTAL MISSIONS THROUGH GLOBAL PARTNERSHIPS $20,000**

Let us analyze the above budget. How much of its $45,800 goes into missions defined as the sending forth of "Christian messengers of the gospel of Jesus Christ who have been called, equipped, and sent forth by the authority of the Lord and the church to cross national borders and/or cultural and religious lines in order to occupy new frontiers for Christ, to preach the gospel of redemption in Christ Jesus unto the salvation of people, to make disciples and to establish functioning and evangelizing Christian churches according to the command of Christ and the examples of the apostles"? Of the $45,800, only $6,000.00 which goes toward the support of Brian Presson[19] qualifies the above definition. All other funds are given to various "ministries", not "missions (M1)." The church has two separate budgets for 2008:

---

[19] I reviewed the prayer letters of the missionaries on the church web site, and concluded that only Brian Presson fits the "missionary" category.

Church budget            $179,200.00
Missions budget          $ 45,800.00

Total budget             $225,000.00

Only $6,000.00 of the total budget of $225,000.00 goes toward "missions (M1)" which represents only 3% of the total budget!

# Christian Finances Today

**Total Income of ALL Christians Globally**
**US$12,300,000,000,000**

**Amount Given to Christian Work**
**1.73% of Total Income**

**Amount Given to Missions**
**5.4% of Total Giving**

## How is the 5.4% Mission Giving Used?

Foreign Missions Giving


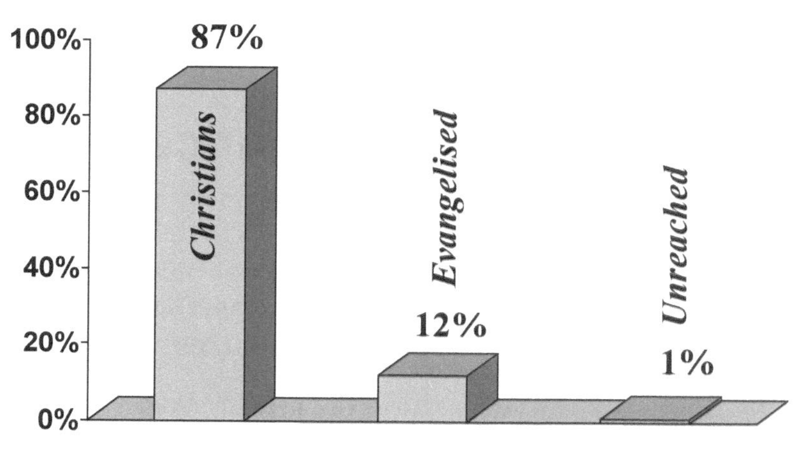

100%
80%
60%
40%
20%
0%
87%
Christians
12%
Evangelised
Unreached
1%

# Percentage Of Christians' Total Income Being Used to Reach the Unreached

1%…    of 5.4%…    of 1.73%

$$= 0.001\%$$

of Christians' Total
Income is being used to
reach the Remaining
Unreached People Groups

## Average Church Budget Spending

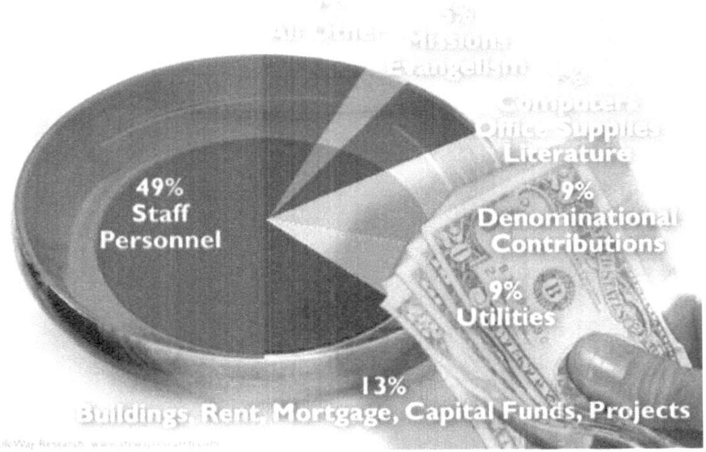

## Faulty Missions Slogans

There are a number of popular missions slogans. They may sound right, but on closer examination, may not be biblically sound. Here are two examples:

*Every person without Christ is a mission field, every person with Christ is a missionary.* This is quite a popular slogan. Every person without Christ needs salvation, but he/she may already have access to the gospel. He/she is not a mission field in the strict sense of the word. Every person with Christ needs to be involved in evangelism and disciple-making, but he/she is not a missionary in the strict sense of the word.

*Across the street, across the seas.* This is one of the popular themes for missions conferences. Does crossing the street to share the gospel with the unsaved constitute "missions?" It is "evangelism" but not missions in the strict sense of the word. Again, the mere act of crossing the seas does not automatically make one a missionary. Unless the person is involved in missionary work as outlined above, he/she is not a missionary in the strict sense of the word.

## Short-Term Missions

Short-term missions is extremely popular nowadays, and missions budgets of many churches have a large percent going into sending young people to foreign countries to do a variety of activities:

- building houses for the homeless
- feeding the hungry
- giving out tracts
- evangelistic concerts
- medical services
- teaching English

and the list can go on.

Many (if not all) the activities of short-term missions do not satisfy the *sine qua non* of missions. True, many of the young people have testified to the spiritual challenges they faced in their lives, and the benefits accrued to them on such short –term missions trips. They testified that they have grown spiritually. Fair and good. If that be the case, do not call those short-term assignments as "short-term missions." Call them as "work" or your church "discipleship" program since those activities are "disciple-making" activities. Neither should those expenses be included in the missions budget.

Many of the short-termers do not know the culture, language and religious beliefs of the countries they are going to. Valuable resources have been wasted.

Short-term "missions" are useful in the context of a long term strategy that satisfied the *sine qua non* of missions. If the short-termers are going to the unreached peoples and places as a first step toward winning disciples for Christ which will eventually lead to the planting of new churches, that would satisfy the *sine qua non* of missions. For example, our students at the ACTS Institute in Western Nepal ventured into an unreached village to preach the Gospel to an unreached people group during the course of their studies, and then one of the graduates was eventually commissioned to go to that village again to disciple new believers, and to plant a church.

## Assignment

Evaluate your church missions budget —What percent of the total church budget goes to M1, M2, and M3? What changes would you make?

# The Missiological God

God's missions originated from His heart. Missions did not begin with the Great Commission of Christ (Matthew 28:19-20). It began with the Great Compassion of God. Missions began with the very heart of God. God's heart was moved to save mankind. Our God is a missiological God.

- When Adam and Eve sinned against God, God provided the first promise of redemption in Genesis 3:15: *"And I will put enmity between you and the woman, and between your offspring and hers; he will crush your head, and you will strike his heel."* The promise refers to the ultimate "Seed" of the woman (Messiah) over Satan (cf. Revelations 19:1-5; Galatians 3:16, 19; Hebrews 2:14; and 1 John 3:8). Most interpreters recognize this verse as the first biblical promise of the provision of salvation (the *protevangelium* or "first gospel").

- When the nations refused to spread out into the world, but attempted instead to build a tower to the heavens, God came down to disperse them. He did not abandon mankind forever. He chose Abraham so the world may be reached again. (Genesis 10-12)

- When His "Seed" was in danger during the time of Abraham's sojourn in Egypt, God intervened to protect Sarah's womb, thus preserving the line from which the Messiah would come. (Genesis 12)

- When His people disobeyed Him, God sent prophets to warn and beseech them to return to Him.

- When His people were on the verge of total annihilation (Esther), He intervened to protect them, thus preserving the line from which the Messiah would come.

- In the fullness of time, God sent His Son into the world (Gal. 4:4).

  *God so loved the world that he gave his one and only Son, that whoever believes in him shall not perish but have eternal life. For God did not send his Son into the world to condemn the world, but to save the world through him.* (John 3:16-17)

- When Jesus saw the multitudes, He had compassion on them. (Matthew 9:36)

- Jesus felt compassion on the needy multitudes. (Matthew 14:14; Mark 6:34) He healed their sick (Matthew 14:14) and taught them. (Mark 6:34)

- Jesus had compassion on the hungry multitudes and He fed them. (Matthew 15:32-38; Mark 8:1-9)

- Jesus had compassion on the two blind beggars, and He restored their sight. (Matthew 20:34)

- Jesus had compassion on the unclean leper, and He healed him. (Mark 1:41-42)

- Jesus had compassion on the grieving widow whose son had died, and He raised him from the dead. (Luke 7:14-15)

- When Christ was nailed on the cross, He prayed the Father would forgive them because they did not know what they did (Luke 23:34).

The above are just a few glimpses into the very heart of God. His compassion permeates the pages of Scripture. No one can read the Word without being touched by His love. From the beginning to the end, His love is from eternity to eternity because He, Himself, is love. (1 John 4:8)

Missions begins in His heart. His compassion moves Him to missions. How about your heart?

Obviously, God's heart was touched by the pain and suffering of humanity. No heart can remain unmoved by the pain and suffering of this world. Jesus was in touch with the reality of human suffering as He lived among man.

Do we want to have compassion in our hearts? Draw near to the heart of God and draw near to the cry of human hearts in pain and suffering. As long as we are sheltered from the painful reality of this world, detached from the suffering of the sick, isolated from the pain of those dying from cancer, quarantined from the leprosy of the human souls, fearful of infection by the AIDS virus, and live in places where people cannot reach us and we cannot reach others, our compassion for people remains frozen, our proclamation remains empty, and our profession of faith remains hypocritical.

Missions does not begin with the commission; it begins with God's heart and our heart because we have been touched by Him, and by the pain and suffering of this world.

The Compassion of Jesus:

There are **five** occasions in the Gospel accounts where the compassion of Jesus is mentioned:

1. Mark 1:41 *Filled with **compassion**, Jesus reached out his hand and touched the man. "I am willing," he said. "Be clean!"*

2. Matthew 9:36 *When he saw the crowds, he had **compassion** on them, because they were harassed and helpless, like sheep without a shepherd. Mark 6:34 When Jesus landed and saw a large crowd, he had **compassion** on them, because they were like sheep without a shepherd. So he began teaching them many things.*

3. Matthew 14:14 *When Jesus landed and saw a large crowd, he had **compassion** on them and healed their sick.*

4. Matthew 15:32 *Jesus called his disciples to him and said, "I have **compassion** for these people; they have already been with me three days and have nothing to eat. I do not want to send them away hungry, or they may collapse on the way." Mark 8:2 "I have **compassion** for these people; they have already been with me three days and have nothing to eat."*

5. Matthew 20:34 *Jesus had **compassion** on them and touched their eyes. Immediately they received their sight and followed him.*

Note: There are also **five** commissions of Jesus Christ (John 20:19-23, Mark 16:14-18; Matthew 28:18-20; Luke 24:44-49; Acts 1:6-8)

# No Other Name

Luke 19:10 "For the Son of Man came to seek and to save what was lost."

*Introduction*

Missions is needed because there is no other name by which one can be saved. *Salvation is found in no one else, for there is no other name under heaven given to men by which we must be saved* (Acts 4:12). There is only one Name by which men must be saved: the Name of Jesus Christ. Therefore, *the Son of Man came to seek and to save what was lost* (Luke 19:10). The verse sets forth several unique distinctiveness of Jesus Christ, the Name by which we must be saved.

**The Uniqueness of the Incarnation – "The Son of Man"**

The Son of Man, the very God incarnate in human flesh. The incarnation (not re-incarnation) of the Son of Man is different from the Hindu doctrine of the *avatar.* The *avatars* are many incarnations of Lord Vishnu. But Jesus was not just one out of many incarnations of the Divine. He is the only Son of God and Son of Man whose one and only incarnation is the central event of all history, whose incarnation explains history and the facts of all life. [20]

He entered time from eternity. The Divine invaded space and time. The uniqueness of the Gospel story of His birth is not merely a story of the birth of a baby; it is the story of how the eternal God became a baby. He stepped into time. His birth is an epochal event in God's calendar. Christmas is not just *sentimental*, it is *monumental.*

## The Uniqueness of His Divinity

Jesus is the Son of Man. Luke uses the term "Son of Man" 25 times in his Gospel. They often speak of the divinity of the Son of Man. The following references refer to the divinity of the Son of Man:

1. The Son of Man has authority to forgive sins. Luke 5:24 *"the Son of Man has authority on earth to forgive sins...."*
2. The Son of Man is the Lord of the Sabbath." (Luke 6:5)
3. He predicted His own betrayal, suffering, death and resurrection (Luke 9:22, 44; 11:30; 17:25-30; 22:22, 48; 24:7
4. He predicted His second coming (Luke 9:26; 12:40; 17:24; 21:27, 36)
5. He fulfills prophecies (Luke 18:31)
6. He is seated at the right hand of the mighty God (Luke 22:69)

Jesus is no ordinary man, like you and me. He is Divine. The divinity of Jesus is testified again and again throughout the Scriptures. [21]

---

[20] Frank Whaling, *An Approach to Dialogue with Hinduism.* Lucknow, India: Lucknow Publishing House, 2000. p. 37.

## The Uniqueness of Historicity – "came"

Jesus "came" to this world.  He broke through time and space.  He came to dwell among sinful humanity.  He, who existed from eternity past, came in human flesh and dwelt among us.  He broke through the gates of heaven to descend upon the earth as a baby in the manger.   It is a historical fact that Jesus "came." Christianity is rooted in history.  Jesus is a historical person.  Frank Whaling says,

> In olden times, Hinduism had no interest in history.  The early literature of India is great in many respects.  But it has one weak spot.  In it there is only very scanty reference to history.  In fact, 'the total lack of historical sense is so characteristic that the whole course of Sanskrit literature is darkened by the shadow of this defect suffering as it does from an entire absence of chronology.'  History was merely a part of the cosmic process which was cyclical and had its source and meaning in Brahma, and therefore history had no meaning in itself.  According to this view, there is no progress within the record of history; history as an independent thing has no significance.  In modern times, historians such as K. M. Panikkar, J. Sircar and others, have redressed the balance.  They have seen the need to put ideas into their context in time, to give importance to facts and chronology, and to erect a philosophy of history for India.  However, it is impossible for them to supply facts where the written records do not give any historical facts.  The real lives of Rama and Krishna, insofar as they were real, are shrouded forever in obscurity due to lack of reliable historical evidence.  Hinduism *has* to emphasize philosophy and mythology at the expenses of history

---

21 For further discussions on the divinity of Christ, please refer to Alvin Low, *Unchanging Truth for Changing Times.*

because of the very nature of the scriptures she has inherited.[22]

Paul Pillai adds,

According to the *Vedic* literature, there is no historical intervention of God, history has no purpose. The world goes on indefinitely and purposelessly. Salvation to the Indian mind is something like coming to a standstill at the center of the wheel while the wheel is still moving. There is in Indian religions no historical revelation and no redemption of creation; there is only the annihilation of creation. It denies the reality of the world; its existence is deceptive, and its appearance purposeless. In this sense the gospel is definitely new and inconceivable for the mind of Indian religions, because of its revelatory nature and historicity of its foundation.[23]

**The Uniqueness of Divine Initiative – "seek"**

Christ came to seek and save what was lost. He took the initiative. This is a uniqueness of divine initiative absent from all the religions of the world. World religions are man's attempt to seek God. But Christianity is unique. It is God seeking man. The Christian faith is not about us going to God, but about God's coming to us in Christ. It is not our reaching God. It is God reaching us. We are not in search of God. God is in search of us. It is not our quest for God. It is God's quest for us in Christ.

In the Hindu doctrine, there is no stress on God seeking men and women. According to the Gita, God will receive all those who go to him in the right attitude of trust, but there is no sense of

---

[22] Frank Whaling, *An Approach to Dialogue with Hinduism.* Lucknow, India: Lucknow Publishing House, 2000. pp. 66-67.

[23] Paul Pillai, *India's Search for the Unknown Christ.* New Delhi: Indian Inland Mission, 1978, pp. 189-90.

God seeking out men and women first. The Gita says, "Even if the vilest sinner worships me with undistracted devotion he should be considered a *sadhu*, for he has rightly resolved. Speedily he becomes virtuous and secures lasting peace. Knowing it for certain, Arjuna, that my *bhakta* never perishes" (9.30-31). The Christian doctrine is that God not only receives sinners, He takes the initiative in going out to find them.[24]

## The Uniqueness of Divine Grace

The uniqueness of divine grace flows from the uniqueness of divine initiative. If it is the duty of man to find God, then we will have to follow a system of works and rules. But if it is God finding us, it is no longer dependent on our works and rules; it is dependent on His grace. Jesus' came to seek and to save sinners and enemies of God. God's grace has been extended to us.

There is a religious sect in Hinduism which considers salvation by grace. It is called *bhakti*. The *bhakti* movement originated in south India that seems to view salvation as only through grace, but the *bhakti* conceived grace differently from the Christian sense. Bruce Nicholls clarifies,

> ... it is a method to merit the grace of God. Grace operates within the framework of the law of *karma* and *dharma* (duty). It does not cancel it. In Christianity grace cancels the works of the law; but in Hinduism it hastens the process of deliverance from bondage to *karma* and the wheel of rebirth. The god Siva who is always associated with grace never annuls *dharma*, but guides the soul more quickly through it.[25]

---

[24] Frank Whaling, *An Approach to Dialogue with Hinduism*. Lucknow, India: Lucknow Publishing House, 2000. pp. 54-55.

[25] Bruce J. Nichols, "Hinduism," in *The World's Religions*. Ed. Norman Anderson. London: Inter Varsity, 1950; repr. Grand Rapids: Eerdmans, 1983, pp. 136-68 (147). Quoted in Sunil H. Stephens, "Doing Theology in a Hindu Context," *Journal of Asian Mission* (1/2, 1999): 191-92.

Sunil H. Stephens adds,

The grace-slanted *bhakti* school proposes salvation through grace alone, without the cross of Calvary. Since all must pay for their own *karma*, then there is no room for anyone else to take upon oneself other's *karma*. Nevertheless, this is exactly what Jesus did: He took upon Himself our bad *karma* and in exchange gave us His good *karma*.[26]

There is a uniqueness of His divine grace different from the world religions.

## The Uniqueness of Divine Perspective on Human Condition
(what was lost)

The Scripture considers all lost. He came to seek and save *what was lost*. God's perspective on human condition is that all have sinned against God. Such a perspective of human condition is absent from other religions.

Frank Whaling comments,

Sin has no great place in Hindu theology because the Hindu does not allow that sin presses hard either upon the life of man, or upon the life of God. Hogg summarizes the first view very neatly, "If MY sin is really to find me out, I must perceive that it is MY sin and how horribly sinful it is. But according to the *karma*-transmigration concept the sin that is finding me out is always the sin the nature of which I have no knowledge because it was committed by me in an unremembered previous incarnations. Such an experience is no moral searching of the conscience." And if sin is not a burden to the conscience of man, neither, in Hinduism is

---

[26] Sunil H. Stephens, "Doing Theology in a Hindu Context," *Journal of Asian Mission* (1/2, 1999): 192.

it a great burden to the tranquility of God. Hinduism has the idea of a gracious God. But this grace is not costly. It is God's ordinary attitude towards man. Even when He is gracious, God stays outside the problems of human life, and the sin of man does not press hard upon the grace of God or upon the life of God. In contrast, the grace of Jesus Christ is a costly grace. Christ agonized for the predicament of man; He wept for the disobedience of man; He suffered for the selfishness of man; and in the end, He died for the sin of man. The emblems of His grace are some nails and some pieces of wood shaped in the form of a cross.[27]

## The Uniqueness of Divine Compassion

Christ came to seek and save what was lost. It is unique in Christianity that we have a compassionate God seeking sinful man and woman.

His divine compassion considers lost humanity as an object of His love. It is active. Eastern religions consider the present human condition as a result of the deeds of previous lives. Therefore, our present condition is due to our own doing. We deserve what we get because of what we did. No one else can help us get out of our present condition. We are irreversibly bound to the vicious cycle because of the law of *karma*.[28] If someone else were kind enough to help me, he/she would be going against the

---

27 Frank Whaling, *An Approach to Dialogue with Hinduism*. Lucknow, India: Lucknow Publishing House, 2000. p. 61.

28 Eastern philosophers argue that we can control our own "fate" by accumulating good karma in this present life. The problem is that the present existence has been determined by countless lives before this present life that would made it impossible to reverse the accumulated debts of the past which he/she has no knowledge of. The Eastern view throws a person into greater despair, and hence a person would be more likely to assume that whatever happens today and the next life will be due to his "fate." It is fatalism instead of triumphalism.

law of *karma,* which melts out the consequences of my past deeds. Therefore compassion is antithesis to the Eastern beliefs. Compassion towards human beings is therefore intervention into the law of *karma,* and one should refrain from such intervention because in so doing one would accumulate bad *karma* for the next existence. It is a dilemma for Eastern philosophers.

The compassion of Christ is unique in Christianity. He was not afraid to break the law of *karma* (if there is such a law) to rescue sinful man and woman from their lost condition. If He broke the law of *karma* (if there is such a law), then Christ is therefore more superior to that law.

Christianity asks, "How can I help?" (future-looking), instead of asking "How did he/she get that? (backward looking)." The compassion of Christ is unique.

## The Uniqueness of Divine Mission

I have never known my own mission in life until after I have been saved, involved in the ministry for many years before finally coming to a realization that God wants me to be involved in the multiplication of Christian leaders for global harvest. I believe that it has also been the experiences of men and women today. Most of us are unaware of what God would want us to be and to do until much later in life. We recognized our mission in life after we have gained experiences, attained maturity, ascertained our passion, and evaluated our gifts. Similarly, religious founders and leaders of yesterday and today recognized their own mission in life at a later time in life. They did not know their mission in life when they were born into this world. Many of them recognized their own mission in life after they had experienced tragedy, or by some other intervention, which spurred them to think of their purposes on earth.

This is NOT the case for Jesus. He knew His mission from the very beginning, at the time of His birth, yea, before His birth.  His mission had long been prophesized by the Old Testament prophets, reiterated by the early witnesses such as Simeon and Anna.  Jesus' recognition of His mission from the beginning of time is unique, unparallel to any human being ever lived.  Because of His sense of mission, He was able to say even in His childhood, "Didn't you know I had to be in my Father's house" (Luke 2:49).  At the beginning of His ministry, Jesus said that His food *"is to do the will of him who sent me and to finish his work"* (John 3:34).  He understood His mission from the very beginning.

He recognized His mission from the very beginning of time, and He stuck to His mission throughout His life on earth. There was no detour.  He focused on His mission – "seeking and saving what was lost" until He was nailed on the cross, and said, "It is finished."  His has a singular mission.  Men and women today, especially during their mid-life crisis will probably change their course in life, or some of us will simply wander through life aimlessly.  We live an aimless life, but Jesus lived a mission-driven life from the very beginning.  He is unique!

*Conclusion*

Jesus Christ is our unique Savior.  Men and women can only be saved by believing in His Name.  Missions is therefore indispensable.

# The Practices of Paul

Paul says, *"Through him and for his name's sake, we received grace and apostleship to call people from among all the Gentiles to the obedience that comes from faith."* (Rom. 1:5)

The motivation for missions is the Name of Jesus Christ. "For His name's sake," Paul says. It is not for the sake of one's own name, or the name of one's organization, church, or denomination. To see the Name of Christ known and glorified must be our motivation for missions. We are motivated because we want the unreached to know the Name of Jesus Christ.

The scope of missions is "among all the Gentiles." Paul will not rest until "all the Gentiles" come to faith in Him. The scope of missions is a global one. We must not rest until the unreached are reached with the Gospel of Jesus Christ.

The goal of missions is "obedience that comes from faith." The disciples were not only won to Christ, but they also obeyed the Lord Jesus Christ.

In order to accomplish his goal, Paul was involved in …

1. Preaching the Gospel,
2. Preparing the curriculum,
3. Preparing pastors, and
4. Planting churches

## Preaching the Gospel

Paul was called to preach the Gospel to the Gentiles. The Gentiles at that time were completely unreached. He would travel from place to place to preach the Gospel of Jesus Christ. Paul says, *"Woe to me if I do not preach the gospel!"* (1 Cor. 9:16) Paul preached the Good News in the synagogue (Acts 9:20), and in the various cities (Acts 14:6-7; 16:10; 2 Cor. 2:12), among the Gentiles (Gal. 1:16; 2:2; Eph. 3:8). He was eager to preach the Gospel (Rom. 1:15). He was compelled to preach (1 Cor. 9:16). It was his *ambition to preach the gospel where Christ was not known* (Rom. 15:20).

## Preparing the Curriculum

In order to prepare spiritual leaders, Paul wrote letters which formed the curriculum of instruction.

| Book | Content |
| --- | --- |
| Romans | Believing & Behaving the Biblical Doctrines. |
| 1& 2 Corinthians | Disorders in the church |
| Galatians | Defense of Christian liberty |
| Ephesians | Doctrine of the church |
| Philippians | Joy in Christ |
| Colossians | Complete in Christ |
| 1 & 2 Thessalonians | Jesus is coming soon |
| 1 & 2 Timothy | Governing the church |
| Titus | Leading the church |
| Philemon | Forgiveness |

Several observations may be made concerning the Pauline curriculum:

1.  There is a correlation between doctrines and behavior. Christian behavior is rooted in Christian doctrines. Doctrines must influence behavior.

| *Doctrines* | *Behavior* |
| --- | --- |
| Romans 1-11 | Romans 12-16 |
| Galatians 3-4 (A Defense of Justification by Faith) | Galatians 5-6 (A Defense of Christian Liberty) |
| Ephesians 1-3 (The Calling of the Church) | Ephesians 4-6 (The Conduct of the Church) |
| Philippians 1-2 (The Example of Christ) | Philippians (The Exhortations to Christians) |
| Colossians 1-2 (The Complete Life in Christ) | Colossians 3-4 (The Conduct of Christians) |

In other books Paul wrote, there is always a mixture of doctrines and behavior. The delineation may not be as clear as the books indicated above. But, one thing is certain. Paul is careful to root our behavior on doctrines.

In the preparation of any contemporary curriculum, the writer must set forth the biblical doctrines, and then demonstrate how the doctrines should transform behavior.

2.  There is a great emphasis on the community of faith — that is, the church. The letters to the churches in Ephesus & Corinth, and to Timothy and Titus deal mostly with the church. It shows the importance of the church, how the believers are to live out their lives

in the midst of their pagan culture. The individual Christian must not live alone. He is not an island to himself. His life is to be lived in a community, in fellowship with other believers to impact their communities for Christ.

## Preparing the Pastors

It is not possible to pastor all the churches Paul planted. He had to prepare pastors to shepherd the flock of God. In preparing pastors, Paul *taught*, *trained*, and *tended* them

1. Teaching the pastors. In teaching the pastors, Paul wrote materials relevant to the ministry of the church:

   - 1 Timothy
   - 2 Timothy
   - Titus
   - Philemon

2. Training the pastors. Teaching involved the impartation of information, but training involves taking the hand of the under-shepherd, helping him go through the process, giving him assignments to do and be evaluated for improvements. Paul not only taught the doctrines to Timothy, he also took the time to mentor him, and to train him. Paul put him side by side with him to learn the ropes of the ministry before releasing him to go solo. Timothy accompanied Paul during the second missionary journey. By the third journey, Timothy was ready to be stationed at Ephesus. One of the ways of training a new person is to bring him along. Paul brought Timothy along during his missionary trips to help him gain valuable experience in dealing with the various issues of the church.

3. Tending the pastors. Pastors do feel discouraged from time to time, and they need encouragement. When Timothy was discouraged, he encouraged him. Paul called Timothy affectionately, "my son." *"Timothy, my son, I give you this instruction in keeping with the prophecies once made about you, so that by following them you may fight the good fight"* (1 Tim. 1:18). See the appendix on "Timothy.

## Planting churches

When Paul went from place to place, he made disciples, and then he planted churches. Paul and Barnabas planted churches in Lystra, Iconium and Antioch, and on their journey home, they *appointed elders for them in each church and, with prayer and fasting, committed them to the Lord, in whom they had put their trust* (Acts 14:23). After his first missionary journey, Paul wrote to the group of disciples in Galatia, and he addressed his letter to the *churches in Galatia*[29] (Gal. 1:2).

During Paul's second missionary journey, he planted several churches:

1. Paul planted the church in Philippi. Lydia and her household were baptized (Acts 16:15). This was the first church planted by Paul in Europe. Paul wrote to the church in the letter to the Philippians.
2. Paul planted the church in Thessalonica (to which he wrote the Thessalonians epistles).[30] Paul and his team were only in Thessalonica for three weeks (Acts 17:2).

---

[29] If the letter was written to Christians in South Galatia, the churches were founded on Paul's first missionary journey. The letter was written after the end of the journey (probably from Antioch, ca. A.D. 49, making it the earliest of Paul's epistles) when the Jerusalem council (Acts 15) convened shortly afterward.

[30] Paul was in Thessalonica for only three Sabbaths (Acts 17:2) and was forced to leave the city for Athens. He sent Timothy back to Thessalonica to find out the conditions of the church (1 Thess. 3:1). He then wrote this letter after Timothy returned,

3. Paul planted the church in Corinth. [31]     He was in Corinth for 18 months (Acts 18:11).

During his third missionary journey, he wrote 1 & 2 Corinthians and the Book of Romans. He wrote *to the church of God in Corinth* (1 Cor. 1:2; 2 Cor 1:1). The church in Rome was not planted by Paul, but he wrote to *"all in Rome who are loved by God and called to be saints."* (Rom. 1:7)

During Paul's third missionary journey, he planted the church in Ephesus (Acts 19:1-26) to which he later wrote the letter of Ephesians. Paul was in Ephesus for 3 years (Acts 20:31).

*Conclusion*

Paul preached the Gospel, wrote the curriculum, prepared the pastors, and planted churches. He has provided us a good model to follow.

---

reporting on the good health of the church. Both 1 and 2 Thessalonians were written from Corinth during the apostle's 18-month stay in the city (cf. Acts 18:1-11). The first epistle was written during the earlier part of that period, just after Timothy had returned from Thessalonica. The second letter was dispatched a few weeks (or at the most a few months) later. Any date assigned will have to be approximate, though probably A.D. 51-52.

[31]Paul wrote 1 Corinthians from Ephesus (16:8, 9), and 2 Corinthians from Macedonia (2 Cor. 2:1, 12, 13; 7:5).

# Why Church Planting?

The local church is a gathering of God's people. By church-planting, I am not referring to building physical church buildings but to the gathering of God's people in a locality for the purpose of

- Worship
- Instruction in the Word
- Fellowship
- Evangelism

The believers sometimes will meet under a  tree, in a simple hut, besides the river, or in the field.  The early church met in homes.

- Romans 16:5 "Greet also the **church that meets at their house.**"
- Col. 4:15 "Give my greetings to the brothers at Laodicea, and to Nympha and **the church in her house.**"
- Philemon 1:2 "to Apphia our sister, to Archippus our fellow soldier and to the **church that meets in your home.**"

The mandate given to the church is to make disciples, and the natural consequence of disciple-making is church-planting because the disciples must be in relationship with other brothers and sisters in Christ. Disciples do not grow alone. To be spiritually healthy, we are to be together in a community of faith -- a church.

Why do we plant churches?

1. Church planting is a consequence of making disciples. After the apostles won the disciples to Christ, they were equipped, and gathered together in a local church (John 14:21-23). Disciples are made in the context of a community of faith. Disciples never grow alone. That is not God's pattern. As we make disciples, we gather them together to form a local church. The disciples cannot be left alone. The disciples always come together in a local context for the purpose of worship, instructions, fellowship and evangelism. Hebrews 10:24, 25 say, *"And let us consider how we may spur one another on toward love and good deeds. Let us not give up meeting together, as some are in the habit of doing, but let us encourage one another-- and all the more as you see the Day approaching."*

2. Christ loves the Church. Ephesians 5:25 says that *Christ loved the church and gave himself up for her.* If the church is the passion of Christ, I want to make this my passion too. We plant churches because the church is the object of His love.

3. The church is the central program of God in this dispensation. The word "church" occurs 114 times in the New Testament. In the Old Testament dispensation, Israel was the center of God's program. In the New Testament, the church is the central

program of God.  The church is *God's household*, and *the pillar and foundation of the truth* (1 Tim. 3:15).  If the church is the central program of God in this dispensation, we want to align ourselves with God's program.

4.  Church-planting provides us with the opportunity to align ourselves with Christ's promise.  Jesus promised that "*I will build my church, and the gates of hell will not overcome it.*"  (Matthew 16:18).  This is a wonderful promise that cannot fail.  Do you want to do something that cannot fail?  This is it.  Jesus has several wonderful promises:

    a.  The church is built by Him – *I will*[32] *build* my church.
    b.  He possesses the church --  I will build *my* church.  No one can claim possession of the church.  He is the originator and the possessor.
    c.  The church is victorious --  The word "build" is further strengthened by the following phrase, "*the gates of hell shall not prevail against it.*"  It is a divine promise – the church will be victorious.  No persecution however great can thwart the purpose and promise of God.

*He will build His church, and the gates of Hell will not overcome it.*  He promises that the church will be victorious.  He never says that the church will be without problems.

---

[32] The use of the future tense "will" at the time when Jesus uttered those words indicates that Jesus foresaw the establishment of the church sometime in the future.  The timing was not stated, but the Book of Acts indicates that the church came into existence on the day of Pentecost.  The church was not found in the Old Testament.  The church is a new organism to be brought into existence after Jesus' death and ascension, and the coming of the Holy Spirit.  The church came into existence on the day of Pentecost.  The new era had begun.

There will be quarrels, disagreements, but ultimately, the church marches on victoriously. Peter Drucker says that it is amazing that the church survives. Thank God that not only it survives, it thrives. *"I will build my church, and the gates of hell} will not overcome."*

5.  The church provides the context for effective evangelism (Acts 2:42-47). In Acts 2:42-47, the early believers were together - they prayed together, they partook of meals together, they fellowshipped together, and they sang praises together. The corporate testimony is the backdrop for effective evangelism. No wonder, Acts 2:47 tells us *the Lord added to their number daily those who were being saved.*

6.  The church makes the practice of "loving one another" possible. John 13:34, 35 say, *"A new command I give you: Love one another. As I have loved you, so you must love one another. By this all men will know that you are my disciples, if you love one another."* It is not possible to love alone (unless you love only yourself). The command to love one another is only possible when disciples are gathered together in a single locality.

7.  The church manifests the manifold wisdom of God to the rulers and authorities in the heavenly realms. *His intent was that now, through the* **church**, *the manifold wisdom of God should be made known to the rulers and authorities in the heavenly realms, according to his eternal purpose which he accomplished in Christ Jesus our Lord.* (Eph 3:10, 11). This is a mystery beyond my own comprehension. The church manifests the manifold wisdom of God to the heavenly realms. The angels praise, and the devils tremble when the light of Jesus Christ is planted. The church affects the scene not only below, but above.

---

Let us ask ourselves some questions. First, is disciple-making that results in church-planting the central focus of our missions? Missions is not just a department of the church. Missions is not just one of the many activities of the church. Missions is not just one of the many programs of the church. Missions is not the afterthought. It should be the focal point to which all other activities are related. If it is to be the focus, then the leadership is responsible for it. The leaders of the church must be convinced of it. The church leaders must be passionate about it. They must lead the church toward it. When Jesus Christ wrote to the churches, He addressed His letters to the pastors (leaders) of these churches. Unfortunately, there are many churches which make missions one of their many programs, worst still, one of their secondary programs. This ought not to be so.

Second, if the church is central to God's program, and church-planting is the outcome of disciple-making, "how about other ministries?"

Many of you are involved in many ministries such as ministry to the poor, orphanages, building schools, medical missions, or micro-enterprises. All these ministries must some how directly or indirectly contribute toward making disciples resulting in the planting of churches. These ministries are important "supportive" ministries. Ultimately, whatever ministry you are involved in must fulfill God's mandate of making disciples resulting in churches planted in places where there are no churches. You may be involved in building schools. How does building schools contribute to church-planting? You may be ministering to the orphans, how does the ministry to the orphans contribute to church-planting? You must be clear in your heart and mind that ultimately, your ministry is going to contribute toward making disciples that lead to church-planting. They are good and excellent ministries, but it is my conviction that all these ministries must move toward one focal point – churches planted.

We are involved in the training of pastoral leaders and church planters, but the "training" is only a means to the end. The training is not an end in itself. The training results in making disciples to plant new churches where Christ is not named.

I would suggest that you select an unreached part of the world. Focus on that area or country for making disciples and planting churches. Other ministries such as orphanages can become supporting ministries, but bear in mind that ultimately you want to make disciples and plant churches. Don't adopt a "hit and run" strategy. Plan to stay long term in an area or a people group or a country. Stay long, dig deep.

Begin to focus on one city, or one country. Don't spread your resources too thin. I know of churches which give $50.00 to this person, $200 to another person, scattered all over the map, and making very little impact. I am not asking you to cut off their support, but you need to have a focus on your missions. I understand that we are to make disciples of all nations. We can think globally, but act specifically. This is how God works. God intends that all people will be blessed, but He began with one people, one nation – The Jews and the nation of Israel. That was and is His strategy.

I advocate staying long, and going deep in one city or one country. I know that short-term missions are very popular nowadays. Short-term missions without long-term strategies have generated a lot of wastage. It is a better utilization of God's resources to have a long-term strategy. Short-term missions must contribute toward long-term missions. Short-term missions must be done in the context of a long-term strategy. As a church, we need to decide on where we want to have a long-term involvement, and then craft short-term missions so that they are in line with long-term strategy. Please don't just send short-term missions team without knowing eventually what you end up with. Many short-term missions bring more headaches to missionaries out in the field than of help. Sometimes, these short-term missions become sight-seeing tours, achieving little results.  Please do not misunderstand me.  I am not against short-term missions.  But I am not in favor of short-term missions without long-term strategy.  In short-term missions, always ask, "How does that contribute to your long-term goal, or overall strategy of the church missions?"  If you cannot or do not have a clear idea to the answer, it may be time for you to evaluate what you are doing.

There are several churches which are doing that now.  For example, the Stonebriar Community Church in Frisco, Texas is focusing on one state in India – training the disciples to plant churches, and they also have orphanages, clinics etc.  They stay focused on one state, they go deep, and they stay long.  Once or twice a year, they send a short-term mission team to that state, to assist the local disciples in training, in ministering to the orphans, in caring for the sick.  Their short-term mission is in the context of a long-term strategy.

Third, what is God's goal for this church?  How many churches do you want to plant in the next 5 years, 10 years?

Fourth, if missions is the making of disciples resulting in the planting of new churches, then many of our missions activities may not qualify as missions.  If you are going to build houses in Indonesia, please don't call it missions; call it "work" or any other names.  Missions specifically refer to making disciples which lead to planting of new churches. You do not call it missions when you build houses for the poor in the poorer section of your own country, you call it "work."  Call it "work" team, not missions team.

May the Lord bless you as you make disciples, and plant churches here, or in a specific country or city in the least reached part of the world.

# The Church and Para-Church Ministries

If the church is the central program of God in this dispensation, then the church is the mediating sending agency for missionaries to the mission field.

> *Acts 13:1 In the church at Antioch there were prophets and teachers: Barnabas, Simeon called Niger, Lucius of Cyrene, Manaen (who had been brought up with Herod the tetrarch) and Saul.*
> *2 While they were worshiping the Lord and fasting, the Holy Spirit said, "Set apart for me Barnabas and Saul for the work to which I have called them."*
> *3 So after they had fasted and prayed, they placed their hands on them and sent them off.*

The final authority of sending forth personnel rests in Christ (Matthew 28:18), and is administered by the Holy Spirit, but the church plays a mediating role.[33] George W. Peters says that "the local congregation of believers stands in a unique relationship to Christ and that the local assembly becomes the mediating and authoritative sending body of the New Testament missionary. This is a vital, biblical principle and we dare not weaken, minimize, nor disregard it."[34]

---

[33] George W. Peters, *A Biblical Theology of Missions* (Chicago, IL: Moody Press, 1972), 218.
[34] Ibid., 219

The biblical rite of laying on of hands is a symbol of deep spiritual and soteriological significance. In relation to ordination, it is an event of serious consequence to the church as well as to the recipient. In this relationship the ordinance points at least in two directions. On the one hand, it speaks of the priority and authority of the church as the mediating sending agency of God. It presents the church as the responsible missionary body assuming her position and place in missions under the authority of Christ.

On the other hand, the rite speaks of authentication, identification, and the creation of a representative by delegation. By this rite the church is publicly authenticating the call of God; she is constituting a rightful and responsible representative, and she is declaring her identification with the representative in his call and ministry. In the person of the ordained individual, the church by substitution goes forth into the ministry.

By the laying on of hands, the church and the individual missionary become bound in a bond of common purpose and mutual responsibility. It is thus not only a privilege and service; it is also the exercise of an authority and the acceptance of a tremendous responsibility. The identification of the church with the sent-forth representative is inclusive doctrinally, spiritually, physically and materially. It is the constituting of a rightful representative who will be able and who is responsible to function as a representative of the church. The church, therefore, by the laying on of hands, declares herself ready to stand by and make such representation possible. This should include prayers and the finances required for such a representative ministry.

It is my solid conviction that the proper exercise of this biblical principle by the churches would do more to boost the morale of our missionaries and the flow of missionary candidates than many other factors combined. Should our young people realize that not only does "my church go with me, but my church goes in my person, stands with me, prays with me, sacrifices with me, and underwrites my support," the challenge would become inescapable. Here is the church's real opportunity, responsibility and challenge to herself and to the young people. Laying on of hands is not a favor we extend, but a divine authority we exercise and a responsibility we assume. A church should think soberly before it performs the act.

The same principle, however, holds true also for the one who receives the laying on of hands. He recognizes the delegating authority of the church, identifies himself with the church, submits himself to the direction and discipline of the church, and commits himself to be a true and responsible representative of the church. He operates within the doctrinal framework and spirit of the church, conscious of the fact that he is a representative of his Lord as well as of his church, to whom he also acknowledges accountability. Any deviation would be made only by mutual understanding and agreement.

Such relationship of mutual identification and loyal representation would certainly do much for missions. It would prove rewarding for the church, the missionary, and the work. It would involve the church more directly in missions, and it would bind the missionary to the church in a healthy and bolstering manner. He would feel neither "independent" nor "forsaken," knowing that he has a home church that has "gone with him into the field," while the church would know that she is actively involved in missions in a representative manner. Returning from the field, the missionary would find a home for his family and a place where he could enrich his life while making a contribution to his home church.[35]

...while the call of Christ comes directly to the individual and there is a sending forth by Christ Himself, a spiritual church will also sense the call either directly or indirectly. And, a humble and spiritually minded individual will gladly submit to the authority commissioning by the local assembly as the representative body of Christ and sustain a responsible relationship to the sending authority.[36]

The above discussion brings me to an important question for the church. How does my church practise its mediating role in sending forth missionaries? Are missionaries your ambassadors at large? You need to think that through. Leaders need to take time to discuss this issue.

The church should be the mediating sending agency. If the church is the mediating sending agency, then the next question is "why the existence and what is the role of the para-church agencies?"

There are several factors which contribute to the emergence of para-church organizations. First, there has been the unbalanced understanding of the doctrine of the priesthood of believers without a corresponding understanding of the doctrine of the church. After the Protestant Reformation, and fueled by individualism of the 19th and 20th centuries, believers venture into missions through their own initiatives and rights. This is good to a certain extent, except that the church is being left out in the cold.

The second factor is the abdication of missions' responsibility of local churches.

---

[35] Ibid., 221-222.
[36] Ibid., 223.

When William Carey wanted the church to go to the heathen in 1785, he was rebuked by a Baptist minister John Collett Ryland, at a local ministerial meeting, "Sit down, young man; when God wants to convert the heathen, He'll do it without your help and mine."[37]

Missions agencies came into existence through default, by the grace of God, when His church failed to carry out her missions mandate.  It is not the most ideal situation, but given the reality today, missions agencies will continue to play a vital role in world missions.  The question is how do we best use the current realities to accomplish the missions mandate.

There are various scenarios:

1.  The church acts directly as the immediate sending agency

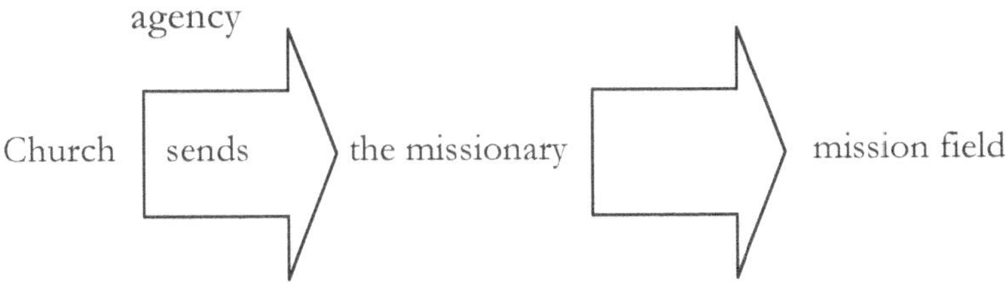


2.  The church sends the missionary, but seconds him/her to the mission agency.

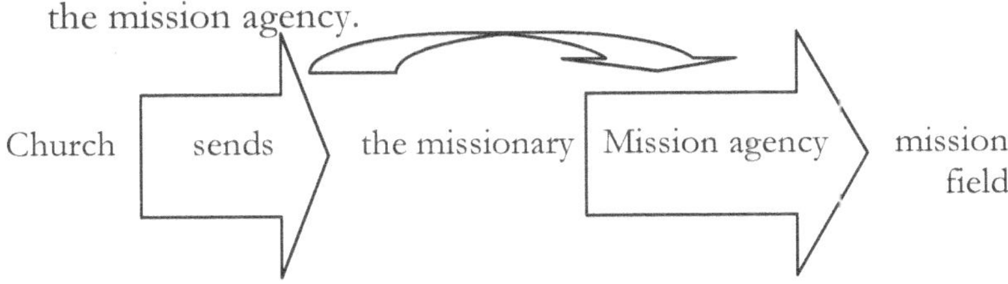


---

[37] Carey had encountered a kind of hyper-Calvinist inertia that, given a comprehensive doctrine of God's sovereignty, asserted a minimalist view of humans' responsibility in advancing God's purposes. If God is willing and able to save, so the position went, why should human beings exert themselves?

This model will require a closer relationship and understanding between the church and the missions agency, and that the missions agency shares the same doctrinal beliefs, values and purpose of the assignment. The secondment "does not relieve the church of the responsibility to care for the missionary. The missionary remains the representative of the church first and foremost, only secondarily that of the society. The church does not sign over the missionary to a society. She delegates the sending forth to a society to whom she is related. The missionary remains a rightful member of the church whom he represents."[38]

This model is best captured by the Pauline word, "partnership."[39] There are various forms of partnership.

3.

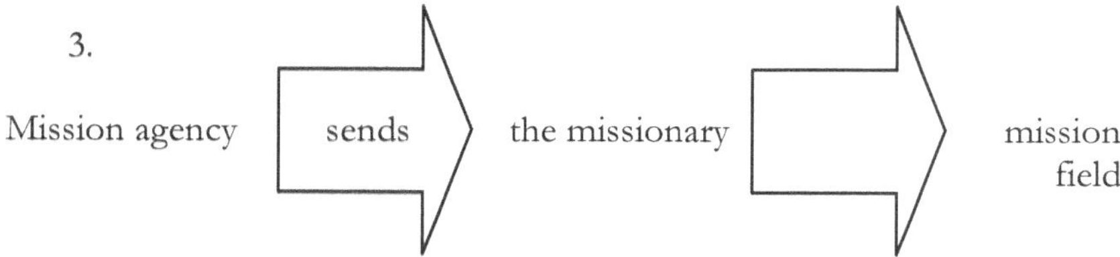


This model is carried out by some agencies without consultation with the local church. To the extreme, it is carried out by bypassing the local church altogether. Or, the church member senses a calling to the mission field, and then he/she goes about finding an agency which is best suited to him/her, often without consultation with the local church. He/she is often not commissioned by the local church. It therefore robs the local church of its primary responsibility, and it spiritual privilege.

There are those who fall in between these three models. Diagrammatically,

---

[38] George W. Peters, 226.
[39] Phil. 1:5, 2:1, 3:10, 4:14. Cf. Rom. 15:24.

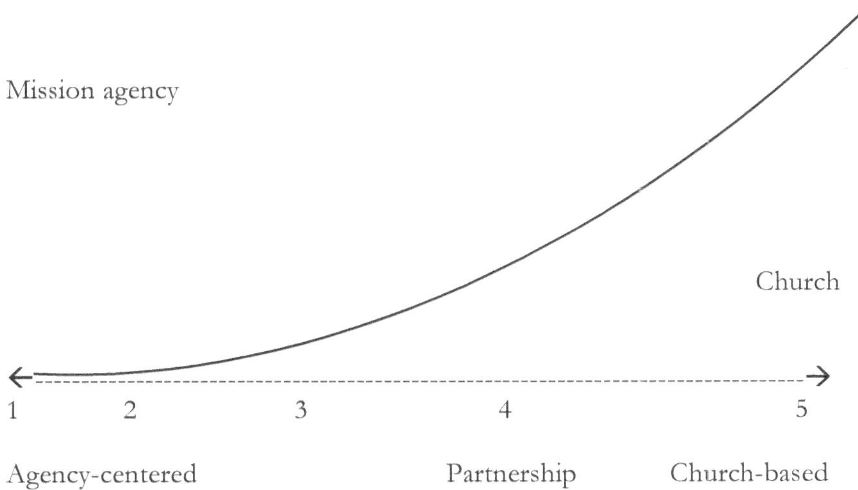


5 = The church sends out her own missionaries, supports the missionaries fully (finances, spiritual etc), supervises the missionaries, and assumes the biblical mandate. The local church's involvement is the highest (This is usually carried out by mega-churches which have resources)

4.5 = The church sends out her missionaries, and then the denomination assumes the responsibilities of financial support, and supervision of the missionaries. (This is done by denominational missions).

4 = The church sends out her missionaries, supports the missionaries partially, but works closely with the mission agencies in supervising the work of the missionaries either through secondment or through some form of mutual understanding. The church's involvement in direct missions remains high (Smaller churches which lack the time and resources will usually adopt this method)

3= The church sends out her missionaries, supports the missionaries partially, seconds the missionaries to the mission agencies, and let the mission agencies have full responsibilities in supervising the missionaries.

2 = The church is made aware of the missionaries, and agrees to support the missionaries either in prayers only, or with minimum support. The church has little contacts with the missions agencies, and usually does not keep up with what is going on in the lives of the missionaries and in the mission field.

1 = The mission agency appoints its missionaries, or the missionaries seek out the mission agency, raise personal support, and the missionaries are sent out to the field without church involvement or awareness.

I would suggest the following procedure for the local church:

    a. Pray for the Lord's wisdom
    b. Study the Scriptures relating to the church and her missions mandate.
    c. Determines the overall mission strategy for the church. Plan a prayer retreat, consultation with many of your own missionaries and workers, and decide which field, city, area, or country that the church wants to have a long-term ministry of making disciples resulting in the planting of churches. The church must have ownership of the missions.
    d. The church prays for workers[40] to fill the needs, or seek out agencies which can assist the church in her strategy.
    e. The church commissions the missionaries, and sends them to the mission field either directly or through an agency carefully selected to fulfill the church's missions mandate.

---

[40] Matt. 9:37, 38.

# The Process of Planting a Church

Churches are to reproduce churches. Like adults who reproduce after their kind, churches ought to do likewise. Unfortunately, some churches are barren, unable or unwilling to reproduce. Couples who do not want or cannot have children have various reasons:

1. They do not want to be inconvenienced. The sacrifice of bringing into the world a baby and nurturing him/her into adulthood is an enormous responsibility which they are not prepared to shoulder.
2. Age - They are still too young to have a baby. Sometimes this is a valid reason if they are still too young, and not prepared for the responsibility of caring for the baby.
3. They have excuses such as being too poor, or too busy.
4. Medical conditions either on the part of husband or the wife are preventing them from having children.

The same reasons can be said of the church. The church is supposed to reproduce after its kind, but they are not because...

1. They are content with what they have. They do not enjoy (neither do they desire) the mess that comes with

planting another church, much less another church among the unreached. They are not prepared to sacrifice their manpower and finances. They do not want to leave their comfort zone.

2. "We are still a young church" "Wait until we grow a bit older." Sometimes this is true, and often it becomes an excuse for inaction.

3. "We are too poor." "We lack the manpower and the money." "We have not reached our city yet, don't think about other villages or cities until we have finished evangelizing our neighbors." "We are too busy with OUR programs."

4. "We are too sick, too many quarrels to do anything else." "We are impotent or powerless in the midst of current challenges facing the church now." "Let us do church planting later, just not now."

We have three children, and we understand that ...

1. Producing a child takes time to accomplish.
2. It requires cooperative effort.
3. We need to "count the cost."
4. We must both accept responsibility for the child.
5. Such an undertaking calls for careful advanced planning.

If you relate the analogy to the church:

1. It was planned from eternity.
2. God counted the cost – the life of His only Son. (John 3: 16.)
3. He paid the price – God gave His Son and Christ gave His life.
4. Jesus is building His Church. (Matt. 16: 18)
5. He requires our cooperation.

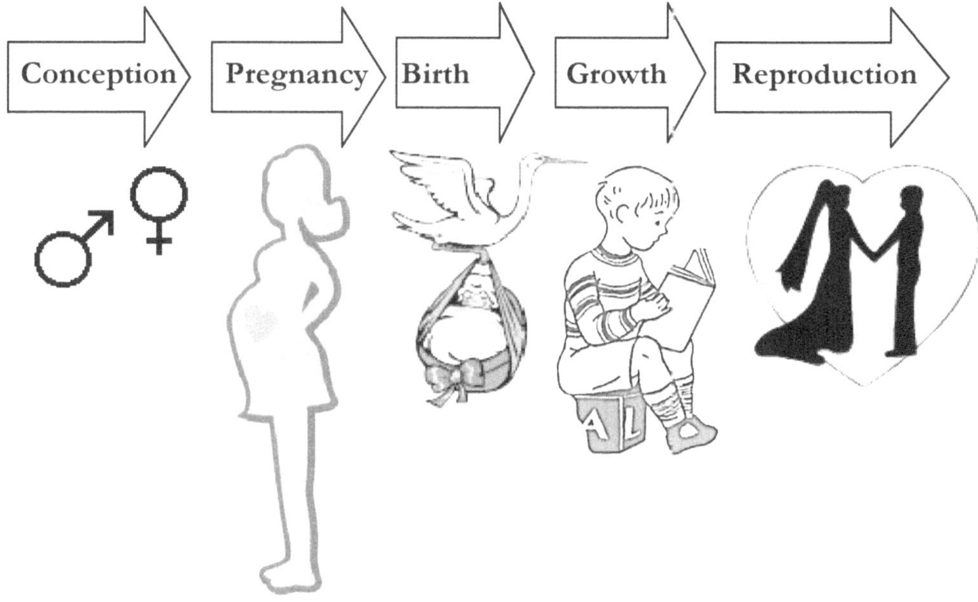


## 1. THE CONCEPTION PHASE

In the conception phase, you receive a vision or a burden from the Lord on reaching an unreached people group or a village after spending time in solitude and in prayer. The vision, idea, desire or burden to plant a new church is "born within us" by God's Spirit.

## 2. THE PREGNANCY PHASE

You carry the vision with you wherever you go. The "vision" continues to "incubate" within your spirit. It is developing, forming, growing like a child within you. You think it through, pray over it, visualize it, and speak about it.

Each time before my wife gave birth, and during the pregnancy, we prepared ourselves by ...

- getting all the food she and the baby needed,
- getting the clothes for the baby,
- preparing the room for the baby,
- checking out the hospital facilities
- consulting with the doctors,
- making sure that we have the funds to pay for the medical expenses,
- preparing a bag with her and the baby's clothes for use during her stay at the hospital so that when the "time" came, we could grab the bag, and go to the hospital immediately.

Just as you prepare for the coming of the baby, you prepare for the birth of your "vision" – planting the church among an unreached people group.  At this stage of preparation -

- you pray for the birth of the new church,
- you pray for wisdom,
- you pray for new converts,
- you profile the people group to whom you are going to reach,
- you prepare materials (such as gospel literature, tracts, Bibles, films)  needed to penetrate into the people group,
- you prepare the funds needed,
- you prepare the team members who are going to assist you
- you prepare for the time to launch the church planting effort.
- you prepare the events needed to launch the church planting effort.

## 3. THE BIRTH PHASE. – Bringing the Church into being.

There are birth pains in bringing the church into being. While the Holy Spirit births new converts and new congregations, church planters partake in the birth pains as they play the role of spiritual midwives.

There are labors involved in birthing the church. It will take time, patience, tears, and prayers:

1. Meeting and befriending people.
2. Praying with those whom you meet when the Lord opens the opportunities.
3. Praying on site with team members.
4. Developing acceptance such as through…
   - Helping neighbors.
   - Coaching a sports club.
   - Teaching guitar lessons.
   - Teaching English.
   - Teaching typing.
   - Teaching basic computer skills.
   - Helping single parents.
   - Helping the aged.
   - Conducting felt-need seminars (e.g. parenting, financial management)
5. Gathering the new believers together.
6. Commencing fellowship meetings.
7. Commencing church services.

Neil Cole advises on finding the persons of peace who are characterized by three things:[41]

1. *They are people of receptivity.* They are open to the message of the person and the pace of Christ.

---

[41] Neil Cole, *Organic Church* (San Francisco, CA: Jossey-Bass, 2005), 182.

2. *They are people of relational connections.* They know lots of people and are an important part of the community, for better or worse.
3. *They are people of reputation.* They possess a reputation whether it is good or bad.

The person of peace becomes the conduit for the passing of the message of the Kingdom to an entire community of lost people. The person's reputation gives credence to the message and becomes a magnet for a new church. There are several examples from the Bible:

1. Lydia was a woman of good reputation. She came to know Christ in Philippi, but her home town was in Thyatira (Acts 16:14), and most probably the church in Thyatira (Rev. 2:18-29) was established as a result of her return there.
2. The Samaritan woman in John 4 had a bad reputation, but after she came to know Christ, she brought the entire village to Him!
3. Cornelius had a good reputation, and his entire social web of relations came to Christ after Peter preached the good news (Acts 11;11-18).
4. The Gerasene Demoniac was delivered by Jesus, and was sent back to his own *oikos* (house) (Mark 5:1-20), so *the man went away and began to tell in the Decapolis {That is, the Ten Cities} how much Jesus had done for him. And all the people were amazed.* (Mark 5:20)

## 4. THE GROWTH PHASE.

As the church begins to grow, there is a need for…

1. Training church leaders in biblical knowledge, leadership, evangelism, discipleship, assimilation of new believers etc.

2. Formation of support/recovery groups to deal with specific challenges such as alcoholics, single parents, etc.

3. Continuing to evangelize the community, and in reaching families and associates. New believers must be encouraged to maintain links with their family members and former associates in order to win them to Christ. This is frequently called "OIKOS EVANGELISM". The Greek word "oikos" is translated "family, kindred, or household." It refers to the close associates of the new believer. Andrew is an example of this style of evangelism. *"Andrew, Simon Peter's brother, was one of the two who heard what John had said and who had followed Jesus. The first thing Andrew did was to find his brother Simon and tell him, "We have found the Messiah" (that is, the Christ)."* (John 1: 40, 41.)

## 5. THE REPRODUCTION PHASE.

A person has not yet reached maturity if he/she is still incapable of reproducing. Similarly, a church has not yet reached spiritual maturity if she is not "reproducing after its kind."

One of the clearest indications of having attained a measure of maturity, having grown beyond childhood, adolescence and puberty, is the capability to reproduce.

When is the reproduction potential introduced? At the moment of conception! But a growth process towards maturity must occur before that potential can be expected to function. So every church has the potential to reproduce, but only those which have moved on to the required maturity will actually do so. The Church is designed by God to grow and reproduce churches.

1. Cultivate a commitment to reproduction. From the earliest possible time members should be taught and made to understand that the church has a commitment

to plant other congregations. They should grow with this awareness in mind.

2. Identify potential harvests. The local church should always be looking for potential harvest areas in which evangelism can occur and a new congregation planted.
3. Encourage evangelism by every possible means.
4. Keep the vision before the people. Church members should be consistently reminded of the mission and vision of their church. They should not be allowed to become introspective and introverted but always aware of those fields which are white already unto harvest.

## Assignment

1. At what stage is your church now?
2. Is your church seeking to plant new churches? If not, why not?

# Profiling the People Group

Research into the people group will give us the facts and valuable information which can be used for intercession and involvement. God does not work in a vacuum. There are examples from the Bible such as that of the spy team sent into the Promised Land (Num. 13-14), as well as in the case of Nehemiah (Neh. 2). God usually uses these information

- to plan,
- to place personnel,
- to proactively meet the challenges, and
- to penetrate more effectively into the people group.

In order to research into the people group, you will have

- to visit the people group in their village/s
- to get a guide to show you around
- to ask questions, and to listen to the answers.
- to re-check information/facts.

Here are several important questions to ask:

*I. Identity*
1.  What is the name of the people group?
2.  What is its closest affinity group?
3.  What is the history of the people group?

*II. Location & Housing*
1.  Where are they located?
2.  Identify it on a map. Which state, district, PIN code?
3.  How far is the place from the nearest village or town? What is the name of the nearest village?
4.  Describe the topography of the place.
5.  What is the weather like throughout the year?
6.  What kind of houses do they live in?
7.  What are their living conditions like?

*III. Demography*
1.  What is the population?
    *   Population by male and female.
    *   Rate of increase of population.
2.  What is the infant mortality rate? Why?
3.  What is he average household size?
4.  What is the rate of migration? Why?

*IV. Language*
1.  What are their languages?
    *   Main written language (if any).
    *   Spoken languages or dialects.
2.  Describe their languages:
    *   Main written language (if any)
    *   Spoken languages or dialects.
3.  Is there a national language required by the government? What is it?

*V. Religious Beliefs & Practices*
1. What is their main religion?
2. What percent of the population adheres to this religion?
3. What are their main deities they pray to?
4. What are their key religious beliefs?
   - What is their concept of God or a Supreme Being?
   - What do they believe about sin? Karma? Nirvana? Re-incarnation?
   - What do they believe about the after-life?
   - What do they believe about man/woman?
   - What do they believe about the beginnings?
   - What do they believe about "punishment"?
   - What do they believe about the "soul"?
   - What do they believe about the supernatural powers?
   - What do they believe about the whereabouts of their deceased ancestors?
   - What do they fear the most?
   - What are some of their taboos?
   - What are their sacred writings?
5. What are their religious practices?
   - Do they have picture/s of their god/s on the wall? What are they?
   - How often do they "pray" to their god/s?
   - What "sacrifices" do the make to their god/s?
   - What rites do they perform during birth, puberty, marriage, death or other key milestones of life?
   - What are some of their sacred objects, shrines?
   - How is their religious worship performed?
6. What are their religious structures?
   - Do they have priests? Or the "medicine man"?
   - What is their role?
   - Are there any religious institution/temples?

7. What are some of their festivals?
   - Are these festivals religious or cultural?  Explain.
   - To whom are these festivals dedicated?
   - How often do they have these festivals?
   - What is the history behind each of the festivals?

## VI. *Arts & Culture*

1. What are some of their art forms?
2. What are some of their favorite drama? Describe.
3. Do they have their own music?
   - What kind of music?
   - What are their musical instruments?
4. What are their favorite dances?  Describe
5. What are some of their cultural beliefs?
6. What are some of their cultural practices?
7. What are their marriage customs?
8. Are there any unusual customs?

## VII. *Occupation*

1. What are their predominant occupations?
2. Are their occupations affected by seasonal weather changes? Explain.

## VIII. *Education*

1. What is the level of their education?
   - Are they literate or illiterate? % of each category.
2. Do the children go to school?  Where?
3. At what age do they begin school?
4. What is the highest standard of education attainable?
5. How do they process information?
6. Is there any gender discrimination in education?

## IX. *Transportation*

1. What is their mode of transportation?
2. Are they nomadic?

*X. Food*
1.  What is their diet?
    * Breakfast
    * Lunch
    * Dinner
    * Anytime in between
2.  Do they observe special diet during special times of the year? Explain.
3.  Where do they get their food supply?

*XI. Family & Social Structures*
1.  What is their understanding about love and marriage?
2.  What is the average age of marriage?
3.  Is the family monogamous or polygamous or serially monogamous?
4.  How do they define a family?
5.  What are their family structures?
6.  Do married children live with the extended family?
7.  Who is the head of the family?
8.  What are the rules of inheritance?
9.  What is the role of the women in the family?
10. What is the role of the husband and wife?
11. Who handles the family finances?
12. How are children being treated?
13. What is their view of divorce?
14. What is the rate of divorce?
15. What is their view of re-marriage after the death of a spouse?
16. How do they relate to the extended family?
17. How do they relate to their neighbors?
18. What kind of communal pressures do they experience?
19. What are some of their social habits?
20. How do they resolve conflicts?
21. Is a member of the family free to choose his/her own religion?

22. What is the crime rate?   What is the predominate crime?  Alcoholism?
23. What are some of their dress habits?
24. What are some of their proverbs (the proverbs can tell you a lot about their worldview, or beliefs)

XII. *Politics*
1. What is the political or government structure within the group?
2. What is their relationship with the regional and/or central government?

XIII. *Christian Missions*
1. Were there any previous missions endeavors?  If yes, explain.
2. Have those missions endeavors been successful?  Why or why not?
3. How many churches are there in the village?
4. How many of them are Christians?
5. Are there churches in the nearby villages?
6. Are there Bibles in their own language?
7. Do they have Christian broadcast programs in their own language?
8. Are there media presentations of the gospel available in their own language?

# Prayer

Prayer is an indication of our dependence on God. A dependent disciple is a humble disciple. Proud people don't pray because they think that they can do the task on their own strength. God's people are dependent people. Therefore, we pray.

Prayer re-orientates us to God. The bigger God is to us, the better will be our perspective on our problems.

## Why pray?

*The Immensity of the Task*

Prayer is an absolute essential in any divine endeavor because of the immensity of the task. We have an enormous task of making disciples of all nations (Matt. 28:19, 20). Jesus recognized the immensity of the task, and He asked us to pray for workers to be sent into the harvest field (Matt. 9:36-38)

*The Inadequacy of our being*

The inadequacy of our being should drive us to our knees. We are inadequate in ourselves. Our adequacy is in God. While

Jesus was praying in the garden, the disciples were sleeping. Jesus said to Peter, *"Could you men not keep watch with me for one hour?"* *"Watch and pray so that you will not fall into temptation."* (Matt. 26:40, 41) Jesus went away again a second time to pray and return to find the disciples sleeping again. The disciples slept again when Jesus prayed the third time. Often, we are like the disciples – tired and weary. We fall asleep when the need is for prayer to strengthen our inner being for the work of the Lord.

*The Invisible force of darkness*

We are warring against the forces of darkness. *For our struggle is not against flesh and blood, but against the rulers, against the authorities, against the powers of this dark world and against the spiritual forces of evil in the heavenly realms.* (Eph. 6:12) Therefore, Paul continued, *"pray in the Spirit on all occasions with all kinds of prayers and requests. With this in mind, be alert and always keep on praying for all the saints."* (Eph. 6:18) The invisible forces of darkness call for prayers at all times. *Your enemy the devil prowls around like a roaring lion looking for someone to devour.* (1 Pet. 5:8)

**Prayer in the Book of Acts**

There are innumerable references to prayers in the Bible, but we will restrict ourselves to only looking at prayers in the Book of Acts as the disciples went forth to evangelize, to edify, and to establish churches.

| Prayer | Results |
| --- | --- |
| They prayed for the coming of the Holy Spirit (Acts 1:14). | The Holy Spirit came (Acts 2). |
| The apostles prayed for the choice of an apostle (Acts 1:24). | Matthias was chosen (Acts 1:26) |
| The early believers devoted themselves to prayer (Acts 2:42). | The Lord added to their number daily those who were being saved (Acts 2:47). |

| They prayed to God after the release of Peter and John (Acts 4:23-31) | The place was shaken (Acts 4:31). |
|---|---|
| The apostles prayed for the "deacons." (Acts 6:6) | The word of God spread. The number of disciples in Jerusalem increased rapidly, and a large number of priests became obedient to the faith (Acts 6:7). |
| Stephen prayed before his death (Acts 7:59). | Stephen was promoted to glory (Acts 7:60). |
| Peter and John prayed for the Samaritans that they might receive the Holy Spirit (Acts 8:15). | The Spirit was given to the believing Samaritans (Acts 8:17). |
| Paul was praying in the house of Judas on Straight Street (Acts 9:11). | God led Ananias to Paul (Acts 9:12-17). |
| Peter prayed for Dorcas who had died (Acts 9:37-40). | Dorcas came back to life (Acts 9:40-41). |
| Cornelius prayed to God regularly (Acts 10:2, 30, 31). | God sent Peter to share with Cornelius the good news (Acts 10:34-44). |
| Peter went up on the roof to pray (Acts 10:9, 11:5). | Peter saw a vision (Acts 10:11-16, 11:5-10). |
| The church prayed for Peter who was imprisoned (Acts 12:5, 12). | Peter was miraculously released (Acts 12:6-11). |
| The church at Antioch prayed for Paul and Barnabas before sending them forth (Acts 13:1-3). | God blessed their first missionary journey (Acts 13-14). |
| Paul and Silas were praying in the prison (Acts 16:25). | They were miraculously released (Acts 16:26-40). |
| Paul prayed with the elders of Ephesus (Acts 20:36). | - |

| All the disciples, their wives and children prayed (Acts 20:5). | - |
| --- | --- |
| Paul was praying at the temple (Acts 22:17). | The Lord spoke to him (Acts 22:18-21). |
| Paul prayed for king Agrippa (Acts 26:29). | King Agrippa did not believe. |
| Paul prayed for Publius' father who was sick (Acts 28:8). | Publius' father was healed (Acts 28:8). |

## The Missiological Prayer

The prayer that the Lord taught the disciples to pray is a missiological prayer.

*Matthew 6:9 'Our Father in heaven, hallowed be your name,*
*10 your kingdom come, your will be done on earth as it is in heaven.*
*11 Give us today our daily bread.*
*12 Forgive us our debts, as we also have forgiven our debtors.*
*13 And lead us not into temptation, but deliver us from the evil one.'*
*14 For if you forgive men when they sin against you, your heavenly Father will also forgive you.*

*Preliminary considerations*

| Our Father in heaven, hallowed be your name. | God is the Father | As a Father, He gives us bread. |
| --- | --- | --- |
| Your Kingdom come. | God is the King | As a King, He forgives our debts and pardons us. |
| Your will be done. | God is the Master | As a Master, he leads us not into temptation. |

1. The Lord's Prayer is not to be repeated meaninglessly.
   *"And when you pray, do not keep on babbling like pagans, for*

*they think they will be heard because of their many words.*"
(Matt 6:7)

2. It is not the prayer of our Lord (Matt 6:12) because the Lord could not have prayed "forgive us our debts." It is the prayer of the disciples. It should be called the Disciples' Prayer.

3. It is a corporate prayer – note the repetition of the words "our" and "us." We are in the family.

*Assumptions*

There are two basic assumptions in this text. The first is personal, and the second is corporate.

1. Personal. When Jesus said, "Our Father in heaven," He assumes that there is a Father and son relationship. There is a personal relationship. In order to call Him Father, we would have to be born into the family of God. We would have to become children of God.

   You cannot be involved in evangelism and missions until you have personally entered into a living relationship with the Father through Jesus Christ our Lord.

   When Jesus appeared to the disciples the night of the resurrection, He told them twice, "Peace be with you." (John 20:19, 21) He assured them of His peace as a result of His forgiveness before He said, *"As the Father has sent me, I am sending you."* (John 20:21)

2. Corporate. There is an assumption that there is corporate unity in missions. The use of the word, "our" or "us" eight times in these few verses (9-13) indicates that we are in missions together.

Nothing has done more harm to the testimony of Christ than the division and the disunity of the church of Christ.

*The Motivation for Missions is the Reputation of His Name*

*"Our Father in heaven, hallowed be your name."* The Name of God is the motivation for missions.

Names are important. When our first daughter was born, we named her Michelle, meaning "Who is like God?" Her Chinese name is Su Li, meaning modesty and beauty.

Our second daughter is named Maisie, meaning "pearl." Her Chinese name is Ann Li, meaning "peace and beauty."

Our son is named Nathan, meaning "gift of God." His Chinese name is Hsien Yong, meaning "manifestation of His glory."

When we named our children, we pray that they would reflect the meaning of their names.

When parents named their children in the Bible, they also hoped that their children would reflect the meaning of their names. Names in the Bible are therefore indicative of characters (Ruth 1:20). When you hear the name Jacob, you immediately know that his name means deceiver, or one who struggles with God. When you hear the name Daniel, his name means "God will judge."

When you hear the Name of God, "I am who I am," it means that He is eternal. He is from everlasting to everlasting. The world may know that God is eternal, not cyclical.

When you hear the Name Jehovah Jireh, it means "God will provide." The world may know that He is the provider of all our needs.

God's names point to His character.    God's Name refers to His entire person – His attributes.

We want people every where to know His Name, to believe in His Name, to understand the meaning of His Name.

Paul considered the Name of God as his motivation for missions.  Paul said that grace and apostleship was given to him to bring about the obedience of faith for the sake of *His Name* (Rom. 1:5).

There are many who do not know His Name.  They know the name of other religious founders, but not the Name of Jesus Christ.

We proclaim His Name because….

- Acts 2: 21 *"And everyone who calls on the name of the Lord will be saved."*
- Acts 4: 12 *"Salvation is found in no one else, for there is no other name under heaven given to men by which we must be saved."*
- Phil 2: 10-11 *"that at the name of Jesus every knee should bow, in heaven and on earth and under the earth and every tongue confess that Jesus Christ is Lord, to the glory of God the Father."*

The motivation for missions must be His Name.  We must not be motivated by our own names, or the name of the bible college, or the name of the denomination, or the name of the church, or the name of an organization.

We are involved in missions because of His Name.  His Name motivates us to go forth to spread the good news.

Personal applications:

1. If we pray that God's name be honored, we must not smear the Name of Jesus Christ. Our conduct must honor God.
2. We must not take His Name in vain.

What is my motivation for missions?  Is my motivation the glorification of His Name, or the glorification of my name?

*The Urgency of Missions is the Restoration of His Kingdom.*

*Your Kingdom comes.*  There are at least two ways in interpreting Kingdom:

1. God's present rule in the world today.
2. Future rule of God on earth at the second coming of Jesus Christ.

Whichever interpretations you adopt, there is urgency involved.  You are urgently asking God to implement His rule on earth, or asking for the Lord to return soon to establish His Kingdom on earth.

If we adopt the second interpretation, we are asking for the Kingdom to be restored on earth.  We are in fact asking that the Lord will return soon.

If we are asking the Lord to return soon, it will have repercussions on missions.  There is urgency.  There is seriousness.  There is urgency in missions because He will soon return.

*The Goal of missions is the Realization of His Will.*

*Your will be done on earth as it is in heaven.*  When I peek into heaven, what would I see?  I would see *"a great multitude that no one could count, from every nation, tribe, people and language, standing before the throne and in front of the Lamb. They were wearing white robes and were holding palm branches in their hands.*" (Rev. 7:9)  It is God's will to have people from every nation, tribe, people and language standing before the throne and in front of the Lamb.

How many nations, tribes, people language have yet to come to know Him in Myanmar?  Nepal? Mongolia? Laos?  Tibet?

*Your name, your kingdom, your will* show that God is a Father, a King, and a Master.

*The Daily Bread is the Provision of Missions*

*Give us today our daily bread.*  God is interested in your food, clothing, house, studies, and friends.  During the New Testament times, the workers were paid at the end of each day.  A disaster brings empty stomachs.  This is no empty expression.   We are totally dependent on Him.  God is not a hard Master.  He delights in giving us our daily bread.

If God, for reasons He only knows, choose not to provide, it is alright because I have already prayed, "Your will be done."

*Forgiveness is the Practice of Missions.*

The next utterance in the prayer is - "*Forgive us our debts, as we also have forgiven our debtors.*"  There will be plenty of opportunities to ask God for forgiveness as you serve on the mission field. Workers may not work together in a team.   There will be personality conflicts, fights over minor issues, quarrels over minor interpretations of doctrines, and disagreements on how things should be done. "Forgive us our debts."  The "debts" is used metaphorically to refer to "sins."  The verse may be translated, "Forgive us our sins, as we also have forgiven those who sinned against us."  Forgiveness is so important that it is repeated twice. Verse 14 says again, "*For if you forgive men when they sin against you, your heavenly Father will also forgive you.*"  Do you notice that we are supposed to forgive those who sinned against us?  The prayer for His forgiveness is contingent upon our forgiving others.  In other words, if you refused to forgive others, the heavenly Father will also not forgive you.  That is serious business.

To forgive others is one of the most difficult things to do especially when you have been hurt deeply, the wounds are sore, and the memory is fresh.  You clench your fist and want to fight back.  To take revenge or at least to get even is human tendency.  If we truly pray and practice this prayer, there will be less headaches in the mission field.  Indeed, we need this prayer more than ever today.

*The Power of God is the Protection in Missions*

*And lead us not into temptation, but deliver us from the evil one.'* If we pray that He will not lead us into temptation, then we should not intentionally put ourselves in a situation that attracts temptation.

The prayer presupposes that we are in a spiritual battle.  1 Peter 5:8 says that our enemy the devil prowls around like a roaring lion looking for someone to devour.  *"For our struggle is not against flesh and blood, but against the rulers, against the authorities, against the powers of this dark world and against the spiritual forces of evil in the heavenly realms."* (Eph. 6:12)

**Practical suggestions**

1. Walk around the village to which the Lord is leading you, and pray for the village as you walk.
2. Use the people-group profile (in the next chapter) to pray for specific needs.
3. Gather a team of prayer warriors to pray with you, and for you.

## A Glimpse of History

The God of history is the God who hears and answers prayers of His people.  Perhaps, the most remarkable prayer movement came from Count Nicholas von Zinzendorf who started the Moravian prayer meeting in 1727 at his home in Herrnhut, Germany. The prayer meeting went on day and night for more than 100 years, and its impact is still being felt today.  That began the Moravian revival, which resulted in thousands of missionaries and evangelists having an impact in Asia, North America, Africa, and Europe. Fifty years before the beginning of modern foreign missions by William Carey, the Moravian Church had sent out over 100 missionaries. The missionaries endured unspeakable hardships. Many died in difficult circumstances, but others came forth to replace them.

The eighteenth-century revivals in America and England were influenced by the Moravian mission and prayer movements. John Wesley was influenced by the Moravians on board the ship in 1735 when he sailed from England to Georgia (U.S.A.) as an Anglican missionary to the American Indians. In Georgia, John Wesley sought spiritual counsel from the Moravian Bishop, A. G. Spangenberg. On his return to England in 1738, John Wesley met Peter Böhler, a Moravian who exhorted him to trust Christ alone for salvation. It was at a Moravian meeting in Aldersgate Street, London on May 24, 1738 that Wesley's heart felt "strangely warmed" while listening to Luther's preface to his commentary on Romans. John Wesley came to know Christ, and became the leader of the Revival in England. Charles Wesley also came to believe in Christ through the witness and prayers of Peter Böhler.

The Protestant missionary movement was born because of the payer of the Moravians.  William Carey was inspired by the Moravians.  He said at a Baptist meeting, "See what the Moravians have done! Cannot we follow their example and in obedience to our Heavenly Master go out into the world, and preach the Gospel to the heathen?'

The day of revivals is not past if only we, the people of God would humble ourselves and pray unceasingly for the outpouring of His Spirit in transforming and empowering lives to advance His Gospel to the end of the earth. There are many more examples of God answering prayers as He unfolds the drama of the ages.

The birth of American foreign missions, and the Awakenings in American history can be traced back to 1806 at Williams College when a thunderstorm drove five students to prayer while huddled under a haystack.[42] Up to that time there were no foreign mission agencies in North America. In 1810 these young men presented a petition to the General Association of Congregational Ministers at Bradford, Massachusetts, which resulted in the formation of the American Board of Commissioners for Foreign Missions. In 1812 the Board sent its first missionaries Adoniram and Ann Judson to foreign missions.

The Student Volunteer Movement started because of the prayer of one student in 1886 when he gathered 21 like-minded students to pray for a movement of missionaries when he was participating at the summer conference of Dwight L. Moody at Mt. Hermon conference grounds at Northfield, Massachusetts, USA.

Operation Mobilisation traces its roots to the prayers of an American housewife. In the 1950s, Dorothea Clapp began to pray faithfully for the students in her local high school. She asked God to touch the world through the lives of those young people. And God answered her prayers! Mrs Clapp gave a Gospel of John to George Verwer, who later gave his life to the Lord at a Billy

---

[42] Today there is a monument on the Williams College campus, at the spot where the students prayed under a haystack, commemorating "The Haystack Prayer Meeting." The inscription begins with these words: "The Birthplace of American Foreign Missions."

Graham meeting. George Verwer became the founder and international director of Operation Mobilisation.

Never underestimate the power of God who listens and answers our prayers. Never be discouraged by the sometimes slow response. God calls us to pray faithfully. The world may be different because you have come before His throne of grace daily.

*12*

# The Reluctant Missionary – Jonah

Jonah was called by God to go from his home country of the Northern Kingdom of Israel to preach to his enemy nation of Assyria during the reign of Jeroboam II (793-753 B.C.; 2 Kings 14:25).[43]  Jonah's hometown was Gath-hepher in Galilee (2 Kings 14:25; cf. Josh. 19:13).  Instead of traveling North East to Nineveh, he ran in the opposite direction to Joppa (Jonah 1:3), found a ship bound for Tarshish, and went down below deck for a deep sleep. His disobedience is indicated by the following:

1.  Jonah 1:3 says that "Jonah ran away from the Lord... to flee from the Lord."
2.  He *went down* to Joppa, and then *went down* to the lower deck to sleep in the midst of a storm.  He must have been very tired to be able to sleep so soundly.  He *went down* to Joppa, *went down* to the lower deck, and finally *went down* into the sea.

---

[43] Gath-hepher is about 5 miles north of Nazareth (2 Kings 14:25, the same as Gittah-hepher (Josh. 19:13) in the tribal territory of Zebulun.  It has been identified with the modern el-Meshed, a village on the top of a rocky hill. Here the supposed tomb of Jonah, Neby Yunas, is still pointed out.

3. Jonah told the sailors that he was "running away from the Lord" (Jonah 1:10), and the storm was his fault (Jonah 1:12).

4. Instead of asking the sailors to return to shore and let him off, Jonah preferred to die (Jonah 1:12). He would not go to Nineveh. Death is better than preaching God's word to the Ninevites. In fact, he wanted to die *three times* in his book. The first time he wanted to die when he was at sea, running away from the Lord (Jonah 1:12). The second time he wanted to die when he was indeed successful in his missions, but he was so discouraged that God changed His mind by not sending calamity onto the Nivevites, that he asked to die (Jonah 4:3 *"Now, O Lord, take away my life, for it is better for me to die than to live."* The third time when he wanted to die was when God sent a worm to chew the vine, and a scorching wind to beat on his head. *He wanted to die, and said, "It would be better for me to die than to live."* (Jonah 4:8) When questioned by God, Jonah replied, *"I am angry enough to die."* (Jonah 4:9b) I am glad that God denied his foolish request, otherwise we would not have an account of his adventure!

The consequences of Jonah's disobedience:

1. He endangered his own life when he asked the sailors to throw him into the sea.

2. He endangered the life of others. The lives of the sailors were in peril. Do not think that your disobedience will not affect others!

3. He got into deep water (literally).

4. He sin was discovered by non-believers. The sailors drew lots and the lot fell on Jonah (Jonah 1:7).

Jonah knew "about" God, but he really did not know His heart. Theologically, he is right on, but practically, he does not live out his belief. He confessed that he was a Hebrew, and he worshipped the Lord, the God of heaven, who made the sea and the land (Jonah 1:9).  He knew that the sea would be calm if the sailors threw him into the sea.  His theology was accurate, but his heart was not compassionate towards those who did not know Him.  The accuracy of his theology can also be seen in Jonah 4:2 where he confessed that God is *"a gracious and compassionate God, slow to anger and abounding in love, a God who relents from sending calamity."*  His theology was evangelical, but his heart was not evangelistic.  He had a big head, but a small heart, like a tadpole. Unfortunately, some of us share his fault.

Instead of compassion, Jonah was angry.  He was angry when God did not bring destruction upon the Ninevites (Jonah 4:4).  He wanted and wished very much for the destruction of his enemies, the Ninevites.  He was angry when God sent a worm to chew the vine which provided him shelter (Jonah 4:9).  He was angry unto death.

We can identify with Jonah.  The Jonah syndrome is very much part of our lives.

1.  Do we really want to see the salvation of our enemies?
2.  Do we know that God does not wish anyone to perish? *The Lord is not slow in keeping his promise, as some understand slowness. He is patient with you, not wanting anyone to* **perish***, but everyone to come to repentance.* (2 Peter 3:9)
3.  Do we have the compassion of God in our hearts? The only way to capture that compassion is to know God intimately, His word thoroughly, and to walk with Him closely.
4.  Are we willing to leave the comfort of home to go to the unreached to preach the Word?
5.  Do we rejoice when the non-believers come to faith in Christ?
6.  Do we wish ill of our enemies?
7.  Do we live out our theology?  Or is our theology mere empty talk?

8. Do we rejoice at His provision, but get angry with God when the provisions are removed?

God is compassionate. He does not want the non-believers to perish. He is loving and gracious. *God is compassionate towards the nations* is the theme of the Book of Jonah. The constraining love of God must become the compelling love in our hearts, driving us to go to the unreached to make disciples, and to plant churches.

God is gracious. Despite the disobedience of His servant, He gave Jonah a second chance. If God can use a disobedient prophet, how much more would He use an obedient servant? God has given us many chances to serve Him, to speak about Him, to venture into the unreached for Him. Don't run away from Him. You may end up in the stomach of a fish!

## Assignment

1. Is God speaking to you today? Be honest. Are you running away from Him?
2. Have you lost your first love? Why?

# Final Thoughts on Church Planting

## Reaching a Whole Nation

Churches which want to be involved in church planting should select a country (such as Nepal), or a state (such as Bihar state in India) to focus their energies and prayers instead of spreading themselves too thin. Be realistic and focus on a geographical region of the world instead of the entire world. I commend the global ambition of churches, but to be realistic, it is better to narrow down the focus to a specific country or a specific state/region. This would be easier to tackle.

Once the country or a state/region is decided upon, map out the country, state/region, and place black dots on unreached villages and people groups to represent the unreached areas. Put the map in a prominent place in the church where it can be seen by members of the church. This is visual and helps to evoke prayer focus. When a church is planted among the unreached, change the black dot into white dot, and put the name of the church and the church planter beside the white dot. In the next 20 years, our prayer is that the black dots will all be changed to white dots. The map gives a vision to accomplish, and it will create a mental and prayer focus for the entire church for the unreached villages and unreached peoples.

## The Pastor and Church Planting

The responsibility of reaching the unreached, and planting new churches should fall primarily on the Senior Pastor.  It does not mean that he cannot delegate the responsibilities to someone else, but it does mean that he is to be the evangelist and custodian of the vision.

It is unfortunate that Senior Pastors are not at the forefront of missions, and churches have assigned missions to a subcommittee comprised of members who sometimes do not have any idea of what missions is all about. The Senior Pastor is ultimately responsible for missions.

## The Holy Spirit and Church Planting

Be sensitive to the leading of the Spirit.  Paul was sensitive to His leading.  When he was prohibited from entering into Asia Minor, he obeyed (Acts 16:6-10), and then he proceeded forward to Macedonia.  In Philippi, Paul met Lydia and led her to Christ. Lydia was from Thyatira (Acts 16:14), a city located in Asia Minor where Paul was previously prevented from entering.  God had a wonderful plan.  The church in Thyatira was planted by Lydia who returned there.

The apostles were sensitive to the Spirit in the selection of the missionaries. *In the church at Antioch there were prophets and teachers: Barnabas, Simeon called Niger, Lucius of Cyrene, Manaen (who had been brought up with Herod the tetrarch) and Saul. While they were worshiping the Lord and fasting, the Holy Spirit said, "Set apart for me Barnabas and Saul for the work to which I have called them." So after they had fasted and prayed, they placed their hands on them and sent them off. (Acts 13:1-3)* They sent the best men out, in step with the Spirit.

The church should therefore gather to pray together, to consult one another, and to discern the leading of the Spirit on reaching the unreached, and planting new churches. The Lord will open doors, and close doors. Be sensitive to His leading.

# Timothy

Timothy was a special person. He was probably timid and introspective, prone to discouragement (2 Tim. 1:7). Timothy must have felt so lonely when Paul was imprisoned (AD 60-62).[44] There was no one else to turn to for encouragement and counsel. Paul was his spiritual father. The only times they saw one another were during Timothy's visits (cf. Acts 28:30, Phil 1:1, Col 1:1[45]). And then he waited for news of Paul's release.

Timothy must have been overjoyed to learn that Paul was released, and he and Titus[46] hurried to see him in Rome. The reunion must have been sweet, but it was too short as they embarked on their journey again. They arrived at Crete, and bade farewell to Titus[47], while both of them sailed towards Ephesus. The journey

---

[44] There are scholars who believed that Timothy was with Paul either when he was imprisoned, or during the end of Paul's imprisonment based on Philippians 2:19-24. But the evidence is not conclusive. They could have planned to meet after Paul's release, and then Timothy would be sent to Philippi for a short while. Apparently, they did travel-together to Asia Minor and then to Ephesus.

[45] Both Philippians and Colossians were written during Paul's first imprisonment. Ephesians, Philippians, Colossians and Philemon were all written during Paul's imprisonment (cf. Eph. 3:1; 4:1; 6:20, Phil. 1:7; Col. 4:10; Philemon 9). Ephesians was written about the same time as Colossians. Some scholars have suggested that Timothy was imprisoned with Paul based on Phil 1:1, and Col 1:1 where Paul's name was mentioned together with Timothy's name (Phil 1:1), and Paul called Timothy "our brother." This may not be proved conclusively. There was no mention that Timothy was with Paul during the shipwreck voyage to Rome. Most probably, the letters (Philippians and Colossians) were written during Timothy's visit with Paul in prison. (William Hendriksen, *Philippians, Colossians, and Philemon*. New Testament Commentary, Grand Rapids, MI: Baker Book House, 1962, p. 44)

[46] Titus was also called *"my true son in our common faith"* (Titus 1:4). Timothy is similarly described in 1 Tim. 1:2.

[47] Paul later wrote the epistle of Titus while Titus was serving in Crete. This paper assumes a chronological sequence of Paul, Titus and Timothy going from Rome to Crete (Titus was left there), and then to Ephesus (Timothy was left there), Paul went

---

brought back fond memories of his previous travels with Paul. About ten years before[48], he had joined Paul at Lystra (Acts 16:1) during his second missionary journey. More than 10 years had gone by so quickly, but the memories of the past were still fresh in Timothy's mind. He had grown older, even though Paul considered him "young."[49] He may be 30 – 35 years "young." Ten years earlier, he would have been just over 20 years old when he first met Paul. Paul became his mentor, and there was a knitting of hearts.

As Timothy re-traced his journeys with Paul, he recalled visiting Philippi[50].... Thessalonica ... Berea[51]... Athens[52]... Corinth[53] ... Cenchrea[54] ... Ephesus[55] .... As the ship approached Ephesus, the breeze welcomed him into the harbor. They met with the church leaders in Ephesus, and then Paul took leave again for Macedonia (1 Tim. 1:3 cf. Phil 2:24). Paul did the opposite during his third missionary journey. At that time, Paul stayed in Ephesus himself and sent Timothy with Erastus to Macedonia (Acts 19:22).

Timothy found himself alone again in Ephesus. Paul said that he had fought the "wild beast" in Ephesus (1 Cor. 15:32). It is quite a task for a young man to face those challenges. Timothy

---

on to Macedonia (1 Tim. 1:3) where he wrote 1 Timothy, and then to **Nicopolis in Achaia (southern Greece, Titus 3:12).** Paul wrote to Titus either from Macedonia or Nicopolis.

[48] Paul's second missionary began in AD 50. Paul was released from prison on AD 62.

[49] 1 Tim. 4:12. Timothy may have been

[50] Acts 16:12-40. Timothy was not mentioned in connection with the experiences and imprisonment of Paul and Silas in Philippi. Possibly because of his youth Timothy was not imprisoned.

[51] Timothy was not mentioned in the account of Paul's ministry in Thessalonica (Acts 17:1-9). Silas and Timothy were left at Berea but they were to join Paul later (Acts 17:15).

[52] Silas and Timothy joined Paul in Athens (1 Thess. 3:1-3). Timothy was sent back to Thessalonica and Titus to Macedonia (Acts 18:5) from Athens.

[53] Paul went to Corinth from Athens. Timothy and Silas joined Paul at Corinth.

[54] Acts 18:18

[55] Acts 18:19

had to deal with heretics who had wreaked havoc on the church in many areas (1 Tim. 2:1 – 6:10) – their conduct in worship, problem with the widows, financial distress, materialism, and a whole lot of other problems. The church was in bad shape.

Ephesus was a prosperous city. Its citizens were captivated by the pursuit of wealth. Ephesus was also a religious city devoted to the goddess Diana. They were taught that *"godliness is a means to financial gain."* (1 Tim 6:5) Wealth was associated with worship. Becoming a Christian was a passport to material prosperity. The greed for material prosperity and false worship have always been like Siamese twins. (Sound familiar today?) Prosperity has often been falsely associated with piety. There was blatant pursuit of wealth under the cover of a religious cloak. The city was under the grip of spiritual darkness and materialism.

Not too long after he had settled in Ephesus, Timothy received a letter from Paul[56]. How refreshing it must have been to his heart to receive the letter from his spiritual father.

Timothy must have longed for Paul to come alongside him, to encourage him, and to co-labor together. His timid nature and the challenges he faced in Ephesus may have contributed to his stomach problem and frequent illness (1 Tim. 5:23). The outward circumstances must have been such a stress to him. Who would not have those physical problems under those challenging circumstances? He must have missed Paul. He may have shed his tears when Paul left him there (2 Tim. 1:4).

With the letter in his hand, he began to read, searching for words of Paul's coming. Unfortunately, his dream was not fulfilled. Paul wrote *"stay there in Ephesus"* (1 Tim. 1:3), and then Paul added that he was hoping to come to Timothy in Ephesus shortly, but may have to tarry long (1 Tim. 3:14-15). Those words

---

[56] Paul wrote 1 Timothy from Macedonia (1 Tim. 1:3).

must have been so disappointing to him.  When would they ever meet again?

Four years later, Paul wrote, *"Do your best to come to me quickly…Do your best to get here before winter."* (2 Tim 4:9, 21).  It was AD 63 when Paul wrote 1 Timothy.  Subsequently, with the outbreak of the Nerorian persecution, Paul was arrested and imprisoned a second time.  When Paul wrote 2 Timothy during his second imprisonment, it was AD 67, a lapse of 4 years.  Four years is a long time to wait to see a person whom you admire and love.

It is against this backdrop of Timothy's personality and service that one would fully appreciate the words of Paul to Timothy when he called Timothy:

- *Timothy my true son in the faith* (1 Tim 1:2)
- *Timothy, my son* (1 Tim 1:18)

And then, during his second imprisonment, Paul wrote:

- *Timothy, my dear son* (2 Tim. 1:2).

*My true son…. My son…. My dear son.*  Those are precious words.  Little words, but meaningful.  Small words, but powerful.  Those words must have meant a lot to Timothy.  Those are emotive words for a person prone to introspection.  *"My dear son…. I long to see you"* (2 Tim. 1:2, 4) were the final words of a man about to be killed.  The second letter of to Timothy was the last letter of his life.  Those words were written before it was too late.

Whether Timothy reached Rome before Paul's death in AD 68 is not known.  I sure hope that he made it.

Paul had spoken of the intimate relationship before:

- *Timothy, my son whom I love, who is faithful in the Lord.* (1 Cor 4:17)  Those precious words were written almost 10 years earlier.[57]  How sweet to hear those words again.
- *Timothy has proved himself, because as a son with his father, he has served with me in the work of the gospel.* (Phil 2:22)  Those words were penned during Paul's first imprisonment.[58]

It is music to a person's ear to be called affectionately, "my true son," "my son," "my dear son," "my son whom I love."  The last phrase, "my son whom I love" is reflective of the Father's relationship with His Son, Jesus Christ.  The heavenly Father called His Son, *"This is my Son, whom I love"* (Matt. 3:17). The love of Paul for Timothy is a reflection of the Father's love for His only Son.  Isn't that wonderful?

How comforting to know of someone who treasures you enough to call you, "my son" or "my daughter"?  Do we have such a relationship with another brother or sister?

Of all the designations that Timothy was called, the "son" is the intimate one.  He has been called:

1. *Timothy, the disciple* (Acts 16:1)
2. *Timothy, my fellow worker* (Rom 16:21
3. *Timothy our brother,* (2 Cor. 1:1, Col. 1:1, 1 Thess. 3:2, Philemon 1:1, Heb 13:23)
4. Paul and *Timothy, servants of Christ Jesus* (Phil 1:1).

Disciple.  Fellow worker.  Brother.  Servant.  But most lovingly, "my true son," "my son," "my dear son."

It is a challenge to us to establish intimate father and son relationship (or for the women – to establish an intimate mother and daughter relationship) either both spiritually, or physically.  I

---

[57] 1 Corinthains was written in AD 55.  1 Timothy was written in AD 63.
[58] Paul's first imprisonment was during AD 60-62.

hope that we will begin to pursue a life long relationship with a few of our juniors whom we can call "our sons" or "our daughters" and pour our lives into their lives, and that they will continue the work of the Lord beyond our life time.

And don't forget to call your son, "my son," "my dear son," or your daughter, "my daughter," "my dear daughter."  It means a lot to them.  It means you treasure them.